t h e

O F F I C I A L

c a r e e r s

H A N D B O O K

t h e

OFFICIAL

ITV

careers

HANDBOOK

Headway · Hodder & Stoughton

British Library Cataloguing in Publication Data
Independent Television Association
  Official ITV Careers Handbook. – 2Rev.ed
  I. Title
  384.55023

  ISBN 0–340–56849–6

First published 1992

Typeset by Wearset, Boldon, Tyne and Wear
Printed in Great Britain for the educational publishing
division of Hodder & Stoughton Ltd, Mill Road, Dunton Green,
Sevenoaks, Kent by St Edmundsbury Press Ltd

CONTENTS

FOREWORD

Television is a complex industry. It requires a great variety of skills; those who work in it come with a corresponding variety of educational backgrounds and experience.

It is also a rapidly changing and expanding industry, with new companies and new opportunities constantly emerging.

This book is designed to help those who want to work in television understand how their aptitudes and talents best fit the available opportunities, and to help them make decisions about the qualifications they will need.

ITV always needs new talent. If you think you have it, happy reading - and the best of luck.

Chairman of Council, ITV Association
Group Chief Executive and Managing Director,
The London Television Centre

The Master Control Room at Central Television (Central TV)

Part One

GENERAL INFORMATION

INTRODUCTION

This book has been designed to answer most of the queries that people considering a career in ITV might wish to ask.

There is a description of each of the main jobs in the industry. Each description gives an idea of the type of work that is done and the kind of person who is likely to be best suited to the work. In most cases there is also a 'Typical Recruitment Profile' listing the qualifications, experience and personal characteristics which are required. The backgrounds of people in some of the jobs are so varied that it is not possible to describe a typical recruit.

The book also contains a number of sections of a more general nature which should provide useful additional information for people who are planning to apply for jobs.

The book is updated approximately every three years to ensure that it keeps pace with a rapidly changing industry. This edition takes into account changes following the awarding of new ITV franchises in October 1991.

▌ *Points to Note*

1 There are variations in the content of jobs between the ITV companies, and the descriptions can therefore only give a broad picture. Some of the variations arise from differences in the balance of programmes made by each company, while others may be organisational differences.

   The larger ITV companies spend a relatively higher proportion of their time making or commissioning dramas and entertainment programmes, etc. These programmes call for more regular use of skills such as make-up, wardrobe and special effects. Smaller companies will in general concentrate more on local news, features, documentaries and current affairs, etc. These programmes call for a high level of skills, but may need little or nothing in the way of make-up, costume or special effects.

   Staff in smaller companies may be employed across a wider range of skills, and may find that as they are working in a smaller team they take responsibility at an earlier stage.

2 There may also be variations in the qualifications required. However, anyone matching the Recruitment Profile should be in a position to apply for a job in any of the ITV companies.

3 No mention is made of salaries as they vary according to local circumstances. Salaries are however competitive for all grades of staff.

4 Jobs of all kinds are almost always offered on a contract basis, i.e. they are for a fixed period of time. This applies not only in ITV but throughout most of the industry. Contracts may be short term, lasting for only a few days, or several weeks or months to cover the duration of a series. Other contracts may be for a year or two, and may be renewable.

5 Jobs in television fall broadly into the following categories: Creative such as Director, Set Designer, Make-up Artist, Technical such as Engineer or Technical Operator and Administrative such as Manager, Accountant, Secretary, Sales, etc.

There is obviously considerable overlap and every creative person needs to feel at home with the technology of television. A Graphic Designer for example will be highly creative but will work almost exclusively on computers. A Camera Operator will need to understand the technical and physical characteristics of lenses but will also need to frame shots artistically. A degree of administrative skill is needed in almost every job.

Despite the high degree of overlap, either creativity, technical ability or administration will dominate any job and it is important to know where your main abilities lie before applying for a post.

6 With few exceptions, there is no set career path into any job and it is difficult to give step by step advice on how to get into television. This may well change by the mid 1990s with the introduction of National Vocational Qualifications. In the meantime, academic qualifications are important of course, and since competition for posts is very intense, it may be the applicant who has most qualifications to offer who gets the job. The exact subject which is studied may be less relevant than the fact that the applicant has demonstrated the ability to pass a GCSE, A level or degree course. Vocational courses are generally the most relevant. The main qualification that is needed is a flair for the job which can be demonstrated either through previous professional experience or through leisure-time activities.

7 There are many jobs which are only available to people with experience in the industry. These include Director, Production Manager, Lighting Director, Floor Manager, etc. When trainee vacancies occur in these areas they are normally filled by people with experience in another production post.

Vacancies for people with no experience in television are generally in administrative areas, journalism (sometimes), technical operations and engineering. From time to time people with no experience may also be employed as trainees in make-up, research, etc.

The number of vacancies for people without experience is · small. Opportunities do occur however, and it is the applicants with determination as well as talent and qualifications who are usually successful.

8 Vacancies for trainees and experienced people can arise at any time and anywhere. It is not usually possible to predict when they will occur.

9 ITV recognises three trade unions – BECTU, NUJ and EETPU, plus the 'talent' unions – Equity, the Musicians' Union and the Writers' Guild. It is not necessary to be a member of a trade union before applying for any job. You will have a free choice of whether or not to join the appropriate union after appointment, or on completion of a traineeship.

10 There are a number of qualities that are needed by anyone working in ITV. These are additional to the personal qualities listed in the recruitment profile.

Teamwork is essential as every production relies on the co-operation of many people, all of whom are expert in their own field. The need for teamwork extends to administrative and managerial functions as well.

The ability to work under pressure is also important as tight programme deadlines have to be met. This may mean that long hours have to be worked at very short notice.

Commitment to the production is another essential quality, especially for people directly concerned with programme making. The completion of a programme on time, within budget, and to the highest standard, is of prime importance.

Communication skills are also needed. It is important to be able to communicate ideas and concepts clearly and persuasively. The converse is also true – it is essential to listen.

11 Staff who are employed in any aspect of programme making, and in many administrative and managerial jobs, must be prepared to work long hours at any time of the day or week, and in any place. Television is not a nine-to-five job, so it can be disrupting to social life. Potential employees should be aware of this before applying for jobs.

12 **The ITV Companies positively welcome applications from ethnic minorities, people with disabilities, and men and women where they are under-represented in particular jobs.**

HOW TO APPLY FOR JOBS IN ITV

The addresses of the ITV companies are shown below, together with the title of the person responsible for recruitment. Job applications should only be sent to the addresses marked with an asterisk (*), which are usually the headquarters or main studio centres. They will also handle enquiries about vacancies in subsidiary offices.

You should have as clear an idea as possible about the kind of job for which you want to apply, and make sure you have the relevant experience and qualifications before making a job application.

Send a comprehensive, but not too lengthy Curriculum Vitae to the company of your choice, and they will tell you if they have any suitable vacancies. Some may ask you to complete an application form. General lists of vacancies are not available. If there is nothing suitable at the time, the company may hold your application on file for a short period, but not usually for more than three months.

The ITV companies receive a very large number of job enquiries and, in order to ease the pressure, they prefer written applications to telephone enquiries.

Anglia Television

Personnel Officer
*Anglia Television Ltd
Anglia House
NORWICH NR1 1JG
Tel: 0603 615151
Other offices/news centres in
London, Cambridge, Chelmsford,
Luton, Ipswich, Northampton,
Peterborough and Milton Keynes.

Border Television

Personnel Manager
*Border Television plc
Television Centre
CARLISLE CA1 3NT
Tel: 0228 25101

Carlton Television

Personnel Manager
Carlton Television Ltd
101 St Martin's Lane
LONDON WC2N 4AZ
Tel: 071 240 4000
Note: This address is subject to change.

Channel Television

Secretary to the Managing Director
*Channel Television
The Television Centre
St Helier
JERSEY
Channel Islands JE2 3ZD
Tel: Jersey 0534 68999
Other offices/news centre in
Guernsey.
Note: The Bailiwicks of Jersey and
Guernsey have legislative
mechanisms which, in effect, mean
Channel Television may not be able
to employ persons who are not
residentially qualified in the
Channel Islands.

Central Independent Television

Personnel Manager
*Central Independent Television
plc
East Midlands Television Centre
Lenton Lane
NOTTINGHAM NG7 2NA
Tel: 0602 863322

Personnel Manager
Central Independent Television
Central House
Broad Street
BIRMINGHAM B1 2JP
Tel: 021 643 9898
Other offices/news centres in
London and Abingdon.

Grampian Television

Personnel Officer
*Grampian Television plc
Queen's Cross
ABERDEEN AB9 2XJ
Tel: 0224 646464
Other offices/news centres in
Dundee and Inverness.

▨ Granada Television

Personnel Officer
*Granada Television Ltd
Quay Street
MANCHESTER M60 9EA
Tel: 061 832 7211
Vacancies and careers information
line ext. 3277.
Other offices in London, and
offices/news centres in Liverpool,
Lancaster, Chester and Blackburn.

▨ HTV

Personnel Manager
*HTV Wales
The Television Centre
Culverhouse Cross
CARDIFF CF5 6XJ
Tel: 0222 590590

HTV West
Television Centre
Bath Road
BRISTOL BS4 3HG
Tel: 0272 778366

HTV Wales
The Civic Centre
MOLD
Clwyd CH7 1YA
Tel: 035255331
Other offices in London.

▨ Independent Television News

Manager, Personnel and Industrial
Relations
*Independent Television News Ltd
200 Gray's Inn Road
LONDON WC1X 8XZ
Tel: 071 833 3000

▨ London Weekend Television

Personnel Manager
*London Weekend Television Ltd
The London Television Centre
LONDON SE1 9LT
Tel: 071 620 1620
Other offices in Manchester.

▨ Meridian Broadcasting

*8 Montague Close
London Bridge
LONDON SE1 9RD
Tel: 071 378 7898
Regional production centres in
Newbury, Maidstone.
News centres – Brighton,
Bournemouth, Basingstoke,
Reading, Dover and Tunbridge
Wells.
Note: This address is subject to
change.

Scottish Television

Personnel Manager
*Scottish Television plc
Cowcaddens
GLASGOW G2 3PR
Tel: 041 332 9999
Other offices in London,
Edinburgh and Manchester.

Sunrise Television

*The London Television Centre
LONDON SE1 9LT
Tel: 071 737 8995

Tyne Tees Television

Personnel Manager
*Tyne Tees Television Ltd
The Television Centre
City Road
NEWCASTLE UPON TYNE
NE1 2AL
Tel: 091 261 0181
Other offices/news centres in
Middlesbrough and York.

Ulster Television

Personnel Manager
*Ulster Television plc
Havelock House
Ormeau Road
BELFAST BT7 1EB
Tel: 0232 328122
Other offices in London.

Westcountry Television

Personnel Department
c/o Brittany Ferries
Millbay Docks
Plymouth
DEVON PL1 3EW
Tel: 0752 253322
Other small offices/news centres in
Barnstaple, Exeter, Penzance,
Taunton, Torquay, Truro and
Weymouth.
Note: This address is subject to
change.

Yorkshire Television

Personnel Executive
*Yorkshire Television Ltd
The Television Centre
LEEDS LS3 1JS
Tel: 0532 438283
Other offices/news centres in
London, Sheffield, Hull, Ripon,
Lincoln and Grimsby, York and
Northallerton.

Note: The ITC (Independent
Television Commission) employs
mostly administrative staff. It does
not employ programme-making
staff.
   The address of the ITC is:
70 Brompton Road
LONDON SW3 1EY
Tel: 071 584 7011

▓ Channel 4

The programmes for Channel 4 are made by the ITV Companies and by Independent Producers. Channel 4 does not therefore recruit programme-making staff. Vacancies are mainly for professional, administrative, technical and sales staff.

Personnel Officer
Channel 4 Television Company Ltd
60 Charlotte Street
LONDON W1P 2AX
Tel: 071 631 4444

▓ S4C (Welsh Fourth Channel)

Personnel Officer
S4C
Parc Ty Glas
Llanishen
CARDIFF CF4 5DU
Tel: 0222 747444
Note: S4C does not employ programme-making staff.

▓ *Careers Information*

Information on working in ITV is available from the ITV companies and from:
The Careers Information Service
ITV Association
Knighton House
56 Mortimer Street
LONDON W1N 8AN
Tel: 071 612 8304

▓ *Where to Look for Job Advertisements*

Nearly all vacancies are advertised internally on company notice boards and staff are encouraged to apply. Many vacancies are also advertised externally, but the method of advertising tends to vary according to the job.

Most jobs are offered on a contract basis, rather than on an established staff basis. Contracts may last for several weeks or months, or perhaps for the duration of a series.

Traineeships

Traineeships (such as Trainee Technical Operator or Trainee Camera Operator) may be advertised in the local press, through the local careers service or through local employment agencies and Job Centres. The vacancies may also be advertised on air on television or local radio. Some traineeships may be advertised in the trade press, the national press and through university and college careers services.

Administrative Posts

Administrative, clerical and secretarial posts are generally advertised locally in the same way as traineeships.

Television Posts requiring Experience

Jobs which require some previous experience in the Industry, such as Producer, Director or Lighting Director, are normally advertised in the trade press. Some publications which are used quite regularly are *Broadcast*, *Television Week*, *Televisual* and *Stage and Television Today*. These jobs may also be advertised on specialist pages in the national press, for example the Media page of *The Guardian*, and the Media and Marketing page of *The Daily Telegraph*. They may also be advertised in Job Centres.

Professional Posts

Professional posts which are not specific to the television industry, such as Accounting, Computing, Engineering, Marketing and Personnel are advertised in the appropriate specialist publications. Examples are *Electronics Weekly* and *Computing* for Computer vacancies, and *Personnel Management* or *Personnel Plus* for Personnel vacancies. These posts may also be advertised locally in the quality national press, and in Job Centres.

Advertising to the Disabled and to Ethnic Minorities

In order to encourage greater numbers of disabled applicants to apply for posts in ITV, specialist publications such as *Disability Now* may be used.

Job advertisements may also be placed with Community Race Relations Councils and publications such as *The Voice* which are aimed at Ethnic Minorities. Traineeships may sometimes be offered specifically for Ethnic minority or disabled applicants.

THE ORGANISATION OF ITV

The Regional Companies

ITV consists of fifteen regional companies, all separately run and independently owned, but working to deliver a co-ordinated output of programmes throughout the United Kingdom.

Each company is responsible for transmitting ITV programmes to a particular geographical region. Many homes which lie near the boundaries of regions will be able to receive transmissions from more than one ITV company since the areas covered by the transmitters have a degree of overlap.

From January 1993 the regional companies are:
- *Anglia Television* – East of England
- *Border Television* – The borders of Scotland and England plus the Isle of Man
- *Carlton Television* – The London area
- *Central Independent Television* – East and West Midlands
- *Channel Television* – The Channel Islands
- *Grampian Television* – Northern Scotland
- *Granada Television* – North West England
- *HTV* – Wales and the West of England
- *London Weekend Television* – The London area
- *Meridian Broadcasting* – South and South East of England
- *Scottish Television* – Central Scotland
- *Tyne Tees Television* – North East England
- *Ulster Television* – Northern Ireland
- *Westcountry Television* – South West England
- *Yorkshire Television* – Yorkshire and Humberside

The map below shows the locations of the various companies. The London area is served by two companies – Carlton on weekdays and

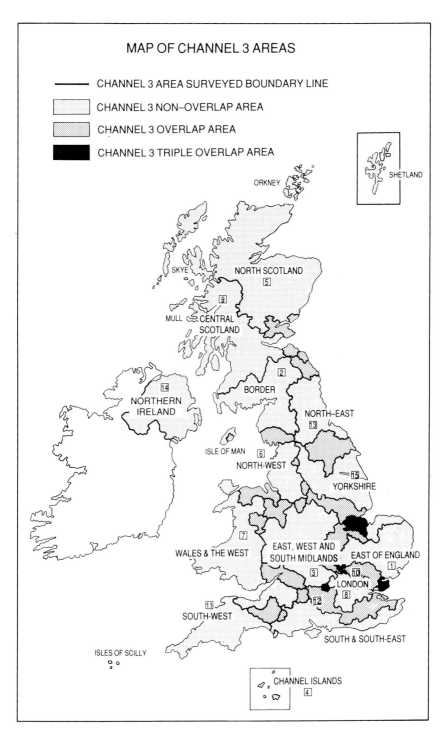

MAP OF CHANNEL 3 AREAS

—— CHANNEL 3 AREA SURVEYED BOUNDARY LINE

CHANNEL 3 NON–OVERLAP AREA

CHANNEL 3 OVERLAP AREA

CHANNEL 3 TRIPLE OVERLAP AREA

SHETLAND

ORKNEY

SKYE

NORTH SCOTLAND
5

9

MULL CENTRAL
SCOTLAND

2

BORDER

14

NORTHERN
IRELAND

NORTH–EAST
13

ISLE OF MAN   6
NORTH-WEST

15
YORKSHIRE

7

EAST, WEST AND
SOUTH MIDLANDS   EAST OF ENGLAND
WALES & THE WEST   1

3   10
LONDON
8

11   12
SOUTH-WEST

SOUTH & SOUTH-EAST

ISLES OF SCILLY

CHANNEL ISLANDS
4

London Weekend Television (LWT) from Friday night to Sunday night. Since London is the largest centre of population in the United Kingdom the potential advertising revenue is sufficient to sustain two companies.

All of the regional companies make their own local news and current affairs programmes. In addition they may all submit programmes of more general interest for consideration for transmission around the network. These programmes may be made in-house by staff or freelancers or they may be commissioned from independent producers.

Each station is responsible for distributing the programmes which it originates. It will send the signal direct to the transmitters in its own region and in addition it will send the signal via BT lines to other stations on the network. They in turn will pass on the signal to their local transmitters. The viewer watching Coronation Street in Sheffield will therefore receive the signal from Granada Television in Manchester via Yorkshire Television in Leeds.

The money for making programmes comes mainly from the sale of advertising time when all other financial commitments have been met. (Some also comes from the sale of programmes). It follows that the larger companies are likely to make or commission more of the expensive programmes such as dramas, and to employ a wider range of staff.

Producer and Publisher Contractors

The chief value of an ITV franchise lies in the holder's contract to transmit programmes to a particular area. This enables the company to sell air time for advertising, the chief source of income for the ITV companies.

All ITV companies are therefore franchise holders or 'contractors' but not all make their own programmes. Those that do are in the majority and are known as Producer Contractors. They will normally employ people with a full range of television skills on a staff or freelance basis.

From 1993 two companies will be mainly Publisher Contractors, that is they will make a minimum number of programmes, preferring to commission most of them from independent producers. Carlton will serve the largest franchise region, but will employ only about 360 staff. It will produce its own news programmes but all other programmes will be made elsewhere. Meridian will make its own regional news and about 50 per cent of other regional programmes, but the rest of its programming output will be made independently. It will employ about the same number of staff as Carlton.

The following table shows the nature of the operation of each company from 1993 and the approximate number of staff employed. The number of staff will be subject to frequent change and may or may not include those employed on contract.

Company	Role	Approximate number of staff
Granada	Producer/Contractor	1100
Yorkshire	Producer/Contractor	1000
Central	Producer/Contractor	1000
LWT	Producer/Contractor	960
HTV	Producer/Contractor	700
Anglia	Producer/Contractor	600
Scottish	Producer/Contractor	500
Meridian	Publisher/Contractor	370
Carlton	Publisher/Contractor	360
Tyne Tees	Producer/Contractor	320
Ulster	Producer/Contractor	280
Grampian	Producer/Contractor	190
Westcountry	Producer/Contractor	170
Sunrise	Producer/Contractor	140
Border	Producer/Contractor	130
Channel	Producer/Contractor	100

Sunrise Television

Sunrise will be part of ITV but it will have a national rather than a regional franchise. It will be responsible for providing a breakfast time service throughout the United Kingdom from 1993. National and international news will be supplied mainly by Visnews, a News Agency, while the ITV regional companies will help Sunrise to provide a local flavour to news. There will be a variety of other programmes including features and family programmes. Some will be made by regional independent producers and some will be supplied by one of the company's major shareholders, the Walt Disney Company. Programmes will also be made in-house.

Independent Television News

ITN is the sole supplier of national and international news for the ITV network (although companies may run their own local news operation, or purchase the service from elsewhere). ITN's position as sole supplier remains until 2003, although it is subject to review by the ITC in 1998. It is jointly owned by the ITV companies, however the Government has stipulated that 51 per cent of the Companies' shares must be sold by the end of 1993. This is a move which is resisted by the ITC and the ITV companies who wish to retain a majority shareholding.

ITN has its own studios at Gray's Inn Road, London and bureaux in Washington, Moscow, Brussels, Johannesburg, Cyprus and Hong Kong. It employs approximately 850 staff including journalists, news crews, engineers and technicians, production staff and management and administrative staff. In addition to its regular national and international news coverage in *News at Twelve Thirty*, *News at 5.40* and *News at Ten* it produces a wide range of other programmes. These include *Channel 4 News*, short news bulletins around the clock for ITV, various news specials when major events occur, and other news-based programmes for ITV, Channel 4 and other customers. With its excellent coverage of events around the world, ITN has an international reputation for reporting news with accuracy and authority.

The Independent Television Association

The ITV Association is the central secretariat of the ITV Companies. It employs about 120 staff who service the committees which formulate industry policy on finance, marketing, industrial relations, training and engineering. There is also a Copy Clearance function which ensures that television advertisements meet the standards laid down by the ITC.

At the time of writing, the Association co-ordinates the work of the Programme Controllers from the ITV companies who compile the network schedules of programmes. By 1993 a new system of programme scheduling will be in operation. It is the intention of the Government that the new system should provide fairer access to the network schedules for all companies which make programmes for ITV. It is likely that an independent Central Scheduler will be appointed to select programme ideas on merit.

There is also a Film Purchase section within the Association which is responsible for purchasing feature films from around the world on behalf of the network. Other departments include ITV Sport which co-ordinates the televising of major sporting events.

Channel 4 Television

Channel 4, which began broadcasting in 1982, has a remit to innovate and experiment with imaginative new ideas, particularly in areas of programming which ITV does not cater for. It serves the whole of the United Kingdom with the exception of Wales.

Until January 1993 it will continue to be financed by subscription from the ITV companies, who in return have the right to sell advertising space on Channel 4 in their regions. From 1993 Channel 4 will sell its own advertising time and become financially independent of the Channel 3 (ITV) companies.

Channel 4 does not make its own programmes but employs a number of specialist Commissioning Editors to commission prog- ramme proposals. These may come from the ITV companies or from independent producers. It follows that Channel 4 does not employ programme makers although there is a small studio which is used mainly for continuity announcements. There are also a number of engineers who are concerned with the operation and maintenance of the studio and the sending of the programme and advertisements from the Channel 4 headquarters to the transmitter.

Sianel Pedwar Cymru (S4C)

The Welsh Channel 4 Authority was established as an independent authority under the Broadcasting Act of 1981 with responsibility for a service of Welsh and English programmes on the fourth channel in Wales. The service consists of about 30 hours a week in peak time of Welsh Language programmes and more than 60 hours of English Language output from Channel 4. The Welsh programmes are provided by HTV, the BBC and independent producers. The service is broadcast on NTL's fourth channel transmitter network in Wales and from January 1993 will be funded primarily by the sale of advertising time. Like Channel 4, S4C does not employ programme makers.

THE 1990 BROADCASTING ACT

During the 1980s, changes in government policy and the recommendations of the Peacock Report led to a radical revision in the way in which Independent Television operated. These changes became law in 1990 and were intended to increase diversity in broadcasting and encourage competition. The main changes affecting ITV were:

The Awarding of ITV Franchises by Competitive Tender

Since ITV has historically had a monopoly of commercial television, no ITV company has ever had the right to hold a regional franchise for an unlimited period of time. In the public interest, franchises (or licenses) have been open to tender after a given period. The former Independent Television Authority (ITA) and its successor the Independent Broadcasting Authority (IBA) were responsible for allocating the licenses to whichever contenders could offer the highest quality of programmes. The Government believed that the system was too subjective. The 1990 Broadcasting Act introduced a more objective system of awarding franchises, which was to be managed by the Independent Television Commission, the successor to the IBA.

All applicants were required to cross a 'quality threshold' by demonstrating they could deliver a certain level of quality programming in their region. They were also required to enter a cash bid payable on an annual basis to the Treasury. The licenses were to be awarded to the highest cash bidders from those applicants who had passed the quality threshold.

The licenses, which were to last for a period of 20 years from 1993, were announced in October 1991. Four of the existing licensees, Thames, TVS, TV-am and TSW were replaced by four new companies: Carlton, Meridian, Sunrise and Westcountry Television.

The size of successful cash bids varied from £1000 a year index linked to about £43 million.

The new license holders will be protected from take-over by other organisations until 1994. Any organisation which then takes over an ITV company will assume the full commitment to maintain quality programming and to pay the cash bid.

The franchise for the Channel 3 Teletext service was also advertised in 1991. It is currently held by Oracle. The service must provide national and international news, regional and public service information.

Central Scheduling and Commissioning

A new obligation was placed on licensees to establish an independent system to administer the commissioning and scheduling of network programmes. This was to replace the system whereby the Programme Controllers of the companies made such decisions. It was the Government's view that the existing system did not give fair access to network schedules to all ITV companies or to independent producers.

The option for franchise holders to be 'publisher/contractors'

Prior to 1991 all ITV companies were 'producer/contractors' that is they made most of their programmes themselves and transmitted them. The Act required ITV companies to commission at least 25 per cent of their programme output from independent producers. This was intended to increase access to broadcast television by programme makers who were not employed by the companies. It also gave companies the option to go further and commission almost all of their programmes from independent producers or other television companies. Those that chose to do so became 'publisher/contractors'.

The Formation of the ITC and NTL

The ITC (Independent Television Commission) replaced the IBA and the Cable Authority in January 1991. Unlike the IBA it is concerned with television services only and is responsible for regulating all non-BBC television services in the United Kingdom. These are Channels 3 (ITV), 4 and 5, cable, satellite and 'additional' services. The ITC has a duty to ensure:

- that a wide range of television programme services is available throughout the United Kingdom and that, taken as a whole, they are of a high quality and appeal to a variety of tastes and interests;
- there is fair and effective competition in the provision of such services.

The ITC does not make or transmit programmes. It licences a variety of different services and regulates them through licence conditions and codes of practice on programme content, advertising, sponsorship and technical standards. It is intended to operate with a 'lighter touch' than the IBA, devolving greater responsibility to franchise holders. It ensures that television companies comply with their obligations through its headquarters and regional staff, and with the assistance of 10 regional Viewer Consultative Councils.

The IBA was responsible for the transmission of the television (and radio) signals from the transmitter to the viewer, and owned and maintained the ITV and ILR transmitters throughout the United Kingdom. The ITC will not have that responsibility. National Transcommunications Limited (NTL), a private organisation, will be responsible for transmitters and transmission engineering and research from 1993. From 1997 NTL will lose its sole right to supply transmitter services to Channels 3, 4 and 5 and will be open to competition.

The Launching of Channel 5

Tenders were invited for the fifth terrestrial (non-satellite) television channel in 1991.

The new channel will be funded by advertising, sponsorship and subscription. It will cover about 75 per cent of the United Kingdom. However a shortage of channel capacity means that it will not be available in various parts of the United Kingdom. Full national coverage can only be achieved if the new franchise holder chooses to provide satellite as well as terrestrial transmission.

OTHER EMPLOYMENT OPPORTUNITIES IN TELEVISION AND RELATED AREAS

The pattern of employment in the television industry in the United Kingdom has changed dramatically in recent times. Until a year or so ago, the majority of people were employed on an established staff basis by either ITV or the BBC. ITV now employs only a core of staff to meet regular, known programme commitments. The majority of its workforce is freelance, as are the majority of people working in the industry as a whole.

This chapter outlines other sectors of the broadcasting, film and video industries which provide employment opportunities. All of these sectors (with the exception of the ITC and Equipment Manufacturers) rely heavily on freelance employment.

BBC television and radio

Competition for posts in the BBC is as fierce as it is in ITV. The nature of jobs and the qualifications required may, however, be different and you should therefore make separate enquiries before applying for posts.

The address to which you should apply is:
BBC Corporate Recruitment Services
5 Portland Place
LONDON W1A 1AA

Cable and Satellite Television

Cable and satellite companies with the United Kingdom are regulated by the Independent Television Commission. They provide opportunities mainly for journalists, presenters, engineers, sales and administrative staff. The majority of programmes are bought or commissioned from independent producers although local cable stations sometimes provide opportunities for local voluntary groups, etc., to submit material. Details of Cable Television can be obtained from your local cable station or:

The Cable Authority
70 Brompton Road
LONDON SW3 1EY

For details of employment opportunities in satellite television contact:

BSkyB
6 Centaurs Business Park
Grant Way
ISLEWORTH
Middlesex TW7 7QD

▌▌ *Independent Production Companies*

Independent production companies, or 'independents' should not be confused with Independent Television (ITV). Their role is to make a wide range of programmes and other visual products, but they do not transmit them to the public. Independents may be commissioned by ITV, Channel 4, the BBC, or a cable or satellite station to make a particular kind of programme that will fit into their schedules. They may also make television commercials, or sponsored videos on subjects such as health or road safety. In addition they may be commissioned by industry to make videos which promote a product. Some make videos for training purposes, indeed the range of activities is endless. Some specialise in a particular field, and some provide a range of services.

The size of such companies varies considerably. A few are fairly large but the majority are small. Many consist of just one creative person who hires in crew and facilities for making the production as needed. Very few independents employ people on a full-time basis. Many former employees of the BBC and ITV have established their own independent companies and the market is full of talented and experienced people who can devise a format for a programme and plan how it is to be made. That does not mean there are no opportunities for newcomers, but it is a business where many companies cease trading within a short time. It is undoubtedly an advantage to have some prior knowledge of the television industry, how programmes are made and how the system operates before entering this field. If you are interested in making a particular kind of programme such as educational television, the arts or natural history, look for the name of the production company at the end of the programme credits. They may well specialise in your area of interest, and may just need the skills you have to offer. Further details can also be obtained from:

PACT
Paramount House
162–170 Wardour Street
LONDON WiV 4LA

Facility Houses

Facility houses (or facility companies) generally provide a service to the same markets as independent production companies. Their role is primarily to provide technical facilities and staff to operate them rather than the entrepreneurial and purely creative input that comes from an independent producer. Some offer studio facilities including cameras, sound, vision mixing, etc. Some offer facilities such as special effects or the duplication of tapes, etc. They may be hired by independent producers who do not have their own facilities on 'dry hire' (facilities only) or 'wet hire' (facilities plus operational crew).

They may also be used by broadcast companies when they don't have the necessary facilities in-house. Most facility houses employ a small number of administrative staff as well as engineers and operational crews. They may also employ freelance crews and technicians from time to time.

There are generally no set career paths to follow into production companies or facility houses, however some previous experience is an advantage. There are also opportunities for young people who can demonstrate genuine interest and talent, and perhaps have some appropriate qualifications but no professional experience.

Lists of facility houses and independent production companies can be found in *Kemps International Film and Television Year Book*, the *Broadcast Production Guide* (a supplement produced by Broadcast magazine), the *Audio Visual Directory* and *Yellow Pages*.

With the exception of *Yellow Pages*, all of these publications are expensive to buy and you are therefore advised to enquire at your local library.

Job vacancies in production companies and facility houses are normally advertised in *Broadcast* or other trade papers, or the media page of *The Guardian* newspaper.

Educational Television

Television is an important medium for teaching at all levels in education. Many universities, colleges and even schools have their own television studios for making programmes. The standard of equipment used for educational television varies enormously from equipment suitable for domestic use, right up to broadcast standard. There are usually only small numbers of staff employed in these units. Most are technical staff, but specialists in educational psychology and learning theory (often called media resources officers) are also employed to help user departments to gain maximum benefit from television.

Industrial Television

Many large industrial companies, and organisations such as the police, Ministry of Defence, etc. have recognised the benefits of closed-circuit television (CCTV) as a means of communicating with their staff. Some have television facilities for staff-training, conferences, promotions, etc. Only a small number of staff are employed, most of whom are technicians.

Equipment Manufacturers

The many companies which manufacture equipment for use in television studios offer opportunities for electronics engineers to work in the development and maintenance of cameras, video tape recorders, sound consoles, vision mixers, etc.

Independent Television Commission (ITC)

The head office of the ITC is in London where mainly administrative and manual staff are employed to regulate all television in the United Kingdom outside the BBC. Regional Officers are employed to liaise with stations throughout the United Kingdom. Further details can be obtained from:
The Independent Television Commission
70 Brompton Road
LONDON SW3 1EY
Tel: 071 584 7011

The Film Industry

The British Film Industry has enjoyed a worldwide reputation for excellence. In addition to home-grown productions, many foreign film makers consider that the technical and production facilities offered in the United Kingdom are the best available. Many films are made by Hollywood Producers using British technicians at British studios.

The permanent staff at studios such as Pinewood and Shepperton are mainly administrative, or are employed in crafts such as carpentry and upholstery. Film Producers generally hire the studio and bring with them a freelance team of film camera operators, sound recordists, make-up artists, etc.

Entry into film production is generally at a very junior level, perhaps as a 'runner', with opportunities for progression for those with talent.

The National Film and Television School runs courses at post-graduate level for people with a demonstrable talent for writing, directing, producing, or photography.

The Jobfit training scheme also provides entry level training for a variety of technical and production posts (see Pre-Entry Education and Training courses).

Independent Radio

Under the Broadcasting Act 1990, the Radio Authority was formed to take over the regulatory role for radio from the now defunct Independent Broadcasting Authority (IBA). It covers all radio stations in the United Kingdom outside the BBC and has a remit to offer more scope for new services, give greater opportunities to broadcasters, and to widen listener choice.

The number of Independent Local Radio stations has increased significantly in recent years, providing opportunities for employment for engineers and technicians, producers, directors, editors, journalists, presenters, disc jockeys, sales and administrative staff, etc.

Recently, two Independent National Radio stations have been launched. One is for a non-pop music service and the franchise has been awarded to Classic FM. The other is for a different service on the AM band. A third license is likely to be offered shortly.

The Radio Authority is also responsible for the licensing of 'restricted services' such as hospital, campus and special event

broadcasting. It is the intention to open up, on a trial basis, licenses to aspiring community radio broadcasters and also to cater for short-term or highly localised commercial applications. This should provide a valuable opportunity for those wishing to enter the industry. Further details are available from:
The Radio Authority
70 Brompton Road
LONDON SW3 1EY
Tel: 071 581 2888

The Association of Independent Radio Contractors
46 Westbourne Grove
LONDON W2 5SH
Tel: 071 727 2646

Print Journalism

There are opportunities for journalists not only in the Fleet Street newspapers but also on local newspapers and on all types of magazine. Some organisations offer their own training schemes and a number of further education colleges around the United Kingdom offer recognised courses in print journalism. These are normally approved by the National Council for the Training of Journalists (NCTJ).

Details of careers in regional and local newspapers (but not nationals) can be obtained from:
The Training Department
The Newspaper Society
Bloomsbury House
Bloomsbury Square
74–77 Great Russell Street
LONDON WC1B 2DA

Details of job vacancies can be obtained from your local or national newspaper or magazine.

PRE-ENTRY EDUCATION AND TRAINING COURSES

There are many courses throughout the country which offer education and training in television. Some are run by the public sector (in colleges, polytechnics and universities), and some are run by private organisations. Some offer practical vocational training, whilst others offer academic study of the media.

The choice is bewildering and it can be very difficult for someone wishing to find employment in television to know which one to choose.

ITV does not officially recognise any courses, mainly because the quality of a course can change overnight if a key tutor leaves, or certain equipment is no longer available. There are, however, a number of courses which are known to the ITV companies and are thought to be of a good standard at the time of going to print. These courses are listed below. Employment cannot be guaranteed on completion of any course, and inclusion in the list does not necessarily mean that the ITV companies recruit from the course.

▓▓ *Survey of Courses for Applicants for Posts in Broadcasting*

▓ Courses at GCSE Level or Similar

Address	Course open to	Qualifications	Method
Performing Arts and Technology School, The Crescent, Selhurst, CROYDON, Surrey CR9 2XE Tel: 081 665 5242	Non-fee paying students aged 14 to 18 years (The school is funded by the Department of Education & Science and the British Record Industry Trust)	National Curriculum leading to GCSEs, A levels and BTEC	The curriculum is delivered through the performing arts, e.g. physics is related to lighting and sound, physical education is related to dance.

25

Courses at GCE A Level or Similar

Address	Course title	Length of course	Subject area
Bournemouth & Poole College of Art & Design, Wallisdown, POOLE, Dorset BH12 5HH Tel: 0202 533011	BTEC National	2 years	Practical self-exploratory covering audio visual design. Options in video, sound and slide tape programming.
Gwent College of Higher Education, Clarence Place Site, NEWPORT, Gwent NP9 0UW Tel: 0633 259984	BTEC HND in Film and TV Practice	2 years	Film and TV theory and practice, animation, computer graphics, etc.
Salford College of Technology, Adelphi Building & Department of Performing Arts, Peru Street, MANCHEST-ER 3 Tel: 061 834 6633	BTEC Diploma in Media and Communica-tions	2 years	

Address	Course title	Length of course	Subject area
Sandwell College of Further & Higher Education, Wednesbury Campus, Woden Road South, SANDWELL, West Midlands WS10 0PE Tel: 021 556 6000	Certificate in TV and Audio Production (to include City and Guilds 770 Media Techniques TV and Video Competences)	1 year	Practical TV production. Design for TV, sound production for radio, TV and audio presentation; technical operations; word processing for autocue; media studies; computers for graphics generation.
West Cheshire College, The Arts Centre, Blacon Avenue, CHESTER CH1 5BD Tel: 0244 377595	BTEC National Qualification in Media	2 years	A communication course offering practical experience and skills in the media.
West Kent College of Further Education, Brook Street, TON-BRIDGE, Kent TN9 2PW Tel: 0732 358101	BTEC National Diploma in Design (Communication: Media Arts Technology)	2 years	Broadcasting/ video/sound/ photography/ film making/ graphic design, theatrical design, audio visual design, etc.

Courses at First Degree Level or Similar

Address	Course title	Length of course	Subject area
Bournemouth & Poole College of Art & Design, Wallisdown, POOLE, Dorset BH12 5HH Tel: 0202 533011	(a) BTEC HND in Photography	2 years	Practical, self-exploratory course covering photography in advertising/ fashion; editorial.
	(b) BTEC HND in Film and TV Studies	2 years	Practical self-exploratory course covering film and TV.
Canterbury Christ Church College, North Holmes Road, CANTER-BURY, Kent CT1 1QU Tel: 0227 762444	BA/BSc Hons: (a) Radio, Film and TV Studies	3 years	The media – theory and practice; in combination with *one* of the following: art, English, geography, history, information technology, mathematics, movement studies, music, religious studies or science.
	(b) Music with Film and TV Studies	3 years	Musical performance, musicianship, acoustics,

Address	Course title	Length of course	Subject area
			electronics, music in the media, etc. Researching, writing and production techniques.
Glasgow College of Building and Printing, 60 North Hanover Street, GLASGOW Tel: 041 332 9969	HND Photography and Video	2 years	Photography and video.
Harrow College of Higher Education, Northwick Park, Watford Road, HARROW, Middlesex HA1 3TP Tel: 081 864 5422 Ext. 4077	BA Hons Photography, Film and Video	3 years	Students study all aspects of film, video and photography in the first year and may or may not choose to specialise in any one area in years two and three.

Address	Course title	Length of course	Subject area
King Alfred's College, Sparkford Road, WINCHEST-ER, Hampshire SO22 4NR Tel: 0962 841515	BA Hons Drama, Theatre and Television Studies	3 years	
London College of Fashion, 20 John Princes Street, LONDON W1M 0BJ Tel: 071 629 9401	BTEC HND in Theatrical Studies Option A, Specialised Make-up	2 years	The specialised skills of the TV Make-up Artist included as part of a wider course.
London College of Printing, Elephant & Castle, LONDON SE1 6SB Tel: 071 735 8484	(a) BA Hons Photography (b) BA Hons Film and Video	(a) 3 years (b) 3 years	(a) Photography. (b) Film and video.

Address	Course title	Length of course	Subject area
Manchester Polytechnic, Capital Buildings, School Lane, Didsbury, MANCHEST-ER M20 0HT Tel: 061 434 3331	BA Hons Design for the Communica-tions Media	3 years	Film and TV production and design.
Napier Polytechnic, Colinton Road, EDIN-BURGH EH 10 5DT Tel: 031 444 2266	BA/BA Hons	3/4 years	Photography, film and television.
North Cheshire College, Padgate Campus, Fearnhead, WARRING-TON WA2 0DB Tel: 0925 814343	BA Hons Media/ Business Management	3 years	Analysis of the media in society. Sound production, photography and video.

Address	Course title	Length of course	Subject area
North Glasgow College, 110 Flemington Street, GLASGOW G21 4BX Tel: 041 558 9001	HNC/HND	1/2 years	Sound and video production.
Plymouth College of Art & Design, Tavistock Place, PLYMOUTH PL4 8AT Tel: 0752 264774	BTEC, HND in Design (Photography, Film and TV)	2 years	Film and TV practice and theory. An emphasis on practical experience.
Polytechnic of Central London, 18/22 Riding House Street, LONDON W1P 7PD Tel: 071 911 5000	(a) BA Hons Film and Photographic Arts	3 years	Theories of art and communication. Theory and criticism. Photography, film practice including technical process.
	(b) BA Hons Media Studies	3 years	Theory and practice of mass communication in journalism, radio and TV.

Address	Course title	Length of course	Subject area
Ravensbourne College of Design and Communica-tion, School of TV & Broadcasting, Wharton Road, BROMLEY, Kent BR1 3LE Tel: 081 464 3090	(a) BTEC HND TV Studio Systems Engineering	2 years	A broad based course in the technology used in the application of Engineering skills when working as a Technician Engineer in TV Broadcasting, radio broadcasting, closed circuit TV, satellite and cable TV.
	(b) BTEC HND Television Programme Operations	2 years	The production areas of cameras, sound, lighting, video tape recording and editing, vision mixing, telecine, audio recording and associated commercial practice.

Address	Course title	Length of course	Subject area
Sabhal Mor Ostaig College of Further Education, Teangue Sleat, ISLE OF SKYE IV44 8RQ Tel: 04714 373	Post Qualification Diploma in Gaelic Broadcasting (SCOTVEC validated)	1 year	Gaelic Television Production
Sheffield Polytechnic, Faculty of Cultural Studies, Psalter Lane, SHEFFIELD S11 8UZ Tel: 0742 720911	BA Hons Fine Arts with Communication Arts option	3 years	Specialisation in second and third years in film, photography, TV for video and small studios.
South West Polytechnic, Drake Circus, PLYMOUTH Devon PL4 8AA Tel: 0752 600600	BSc Hons Electrical and Electronic Engineering	3 years	

Address	Course title	Length of course	Subject area
Trinity & All Saints Colleges, Brownberrie Lane, Horsforth, LEEDS, West Yorkshire LS18 5HD Tel: 0532 584341	BA in Public Media	3 years	A communication course with film and TV options.
The University of Ulster, Coleraine, Cromor Road, COUNTY LONDON-DERRY BT52 1SA Tel: 0265 44141	BA Hons Degree in Media Studies	3 years	Film, television (including video animation) and radio with one third of the course practically based.
University of London, Goldsmiths College, Lewisham Way, New Cross, LONDON SE14 6NW Tel: 081 692 7171	Joint subject Degree in Communications Studies with Sociology or Anthropology or Single Subject Degree in Communications	3 years	Theoretical basis of communications, plus practice in film, TV, radio, journalism, electronic graphics or photography (students opt to specialise in one of the above).

Address	Course title	Length of course	Subject area
University of Surrey, GUILD-FORD, Surrey TU2 5XH Tel: 0483 300800	BMus. Music Tonmeister	4 years	Music, physics of sound, electronics, electro-acoustics, recording techniques.
West Surrey College of Art and Design, Falkner Road, FARNHAM, Surrey GU9 7DS Tel: 0252 722441	BA Hons in Photography, Film & Video Animation	3 years	Photography, film and video animation.

Courses at Post-graduate Level or Equivalent

Address	Course title	Length of course	Subject area
Bournemouth & Poole College of Art & Design, Wallisdown, POOLE, Dorset BH12 5HH Tel: 0202 533011	Advanced Diploma in Media Production. Options in (a) Film and TV (b) Multi-Media	1 year	Practical, self-exploratory course for people with a degree or BTEC HND in photography or film and television.

Address	Course title	Length of course	Subject area
Centre for Journalism Studies, University of Wales College of Cardiff, Park Place, CARDIFF CF1 3AS Tel: 0222 874786	Post-graduate Diploma in Journalism Studies	1 year	Practical journalism course includes broadcast specialism. Regular production days in Centre for Journalism Studies' own radio and TV Studios. NCTBJ* approved.
Duncan of Jordanstone College of Art, 13 Perth Road, DUNDEE DD1 4HT Tel: 0382 23261	(a) Post-graduate Diploma in Electronic Imaging	1 year	Application of micro-electronic techniques to manipulative images.
	(b) MSc (in conjunction with Napier Polytechnic)	1 year	Film and television production.
Falmouth School of Art & Design, Wood Lane, FAL-MOUTH, Cornwall TR11 4RA Tel: 0326 211077	Post-graduate Diploma in Radio Journalism	1 year	Radio journalism NCTBJ* and CNAA approved.

Address	Course title	Length of course	Subject area
Glasgow Polytechnic, 70 Cowcaddens Road, GLASGOW G4 0BA Tel: 041 331 3000	Post-graduate Diploma in Journalism	1 year	Journalism including broadcast journalism.
Highbury College of Technology, Dovercourt Road, Cosham, PORTS-MOUTH PO6 2SA Tel: 0705 383131	NCTBJ* Diploma in Broadcast Journalism. (Exceptional non-graduates with relevant industrial experience may be considered)	1 year	News gathering, Radio and TV reporting, editing, broadcasting, media law, etc.
Lancashire Polytechnic, PRESTON PR1 2TQ Tel: 0772 201201	Post-graduate Diploma in Radio and TV Jounalism	1 year	News gathering, reporting, editing, broadcasting, etc. NCTBJ* approved.
London College of Printing, Elephant & Castle, LONDON SE1 6SB Tel: 071 735 8484	(1) Post-graduate Diploma in Radio and Television Journalism, Newspaper Journalism	1 year	Writing for radio, radio speech techniques, interviewing and reporting methods, the use of broadcast

Address	Course title	Length of course	Subject area
			equipment, etc. NCTBJ* approved.
	(2) CNNA PG Diploma in Scriptwriting for Film and TV	2 years part-time	Research and scriptwriting.
Middlesex Polytechnic, Cat Hill, BARNET, Herts EN4 8HT Tel: 081 368 1299	Post-graduate Diploma in Video	1 year	Video production.
Napier Polytechnic, Colinton Road, EDIN-BURGH EH10 5DT Tel: 031 444 2266	MSc (in conjunction with Duncan of Jordanstone College of Art)	1 year	Film and television production.
National Film & Television School, Beaconsfield Studios, Station Road, BEACONS-FIELD, Bucks HP9 1LG	Associateship of National Film & Television School	3 years	All aspects of film and television production, including writing, direction, producing, camera operating,

Address	Course title	Length of course	Subject area
Tel: 04946 71234			editing, lighting, sound.
Polytechnic of Central London, 18/22 Riding House Street, LONDON W1P 7PD Tel: 071 911 5000	(a) Post-graduate Diploma in Film Studies	2 years part-time	Theory and criticism of film.
	(b) MA in Film Studies	1 year part-time	
Royal College of Art, Kensington Gore, LONDON SW7 2EU Tel: 071 584 5020	MA Film and TV Production	3 years	Film and TV Production.
University of Bristol, 29 Park Row, BRISTOL BS1 5LT Tel: 0272 303 204	Post-graduate Certificate in Radio, Film and Television	1 year	Intensive course in film and TV, plus production of audio and videotape.

*Note: NCTBJ refers to the National Council for the Training of Broadcast Journalists. This is a joint employer, trade union, education sector body which approves courses in broadcast journalism which meet its standards.

Full details of these courses can be obtained from the addresses shown.

All of the courses listed are in the public sector. This does not mean that there are not some worthwhile courses which are run by private organisations, however it is wise to exercise caution when choosing any course.

Some of the questions which are worth asking are:

1 *Is the course vocational, academic or both?* A vocational course should give you practical skills which will enable you to do a job in the television industry such as editing or sound etc. An academic course should develop your appreciation of television as a medium of communication through discussion and analysis. Each has its role to play, but it is important that students should understand from the outset what the course is offering. A vocational course may help you to find your first job more easily (although you will still need to be trained after appointment in the company's ways of operation). An academic course may help you in the longer term to develop your career in the creative side of the industry, but you will require more practical training before or after appointment to a job.

2 *Who are the Tutors on the course?* Do they have professional experience in the Industry? This is particularly relevant for vocational courses. It is worth remembering however that experience in the Industry does not necessarily mean that the tutors were successful at their work, or that they are good at passing on their knowledge and skill to others. A 'big name' guest tutor who visits for two hours is no substitute for a first class course tutor.

3 *What equipment is available?* Again, this is particularly relevant to vocational courses. Whilst it is not essential to learn on 'state of the art' equipment, most of the facilities should be of broadcast standard if the course claims to equip you to work in the broadcast television industry.

4 *How much time does each student spend on the equipment?* Some training courses do not have their own equipment, but book time on a particular piece of machinery at a facility house. This is expensive, and may leave little time for all students to gain sufficient 'hands-on' experience.

5 *What technical support is available?* Is there engineering support on hand if the equipment fails, or are you likely to waste valuable time waiting for it to be repaired?

6 *How much does the course cost?* Does it offer value for money? Television equipment is very expensive, and any course which offers hands-on experience will also be very expensive, unless it is

run at a college or university. Courses in the private sector can cost several thousand pounds and there is, therefore, all the more reason to check that you are getting value for money. Speak to people who have attended the course if you can, and check with the Personnel or Training Department at the local television stations to see if they know of the course.

Industry-based Training Schemes

The growth of the freelance sector of the industry has led to a number of training schemes which offer a broad-based training for those entering the industry. These include:

Jobfit

Jobfit is a two year basic training scheme for freelance technical and production grades in the film and television industries. It combines attachments to independent film and television productions with periods of off-the-job training at the National Film and Television School and Ravensbourne College. Trainees gain broad experience in pre-production, production and post-production. In their second year they specialise in their preferred area such as editing, sound or cameras. No particular qualifications are specified and there is no rigid age limit. Competition is intense for the twenty or so places offered each year. For details write to:
The Administrator
Jobfit
4th Floor
5 Dean Street
LONDON W1V 5RN
Tel: 071 734 5141

Cyfle

Cyfle was set up to meet the need for Welsh speaking technicians in the freelance film and television sector in Wales. Training is in the form of an apprenticeship where trainees are attached to various productions over a two-year period. The ability to speak Welsh is essential, or if not proficient in the Welsh language applicants will

have shown the initiative to learn. This scheme is sponsored by S4C, TAC (Welsh Independent Producers), and the trade union BECTU. For details write to:
Cyfle Cyf
Gronant
Penrallt
Isaf
CARNARVON LL55 1NW

The Scottish Film Training Trust – Film and Video Technician Training Scheme

This one year scheme aims to train freelance assistant camera operators, editors, sound recordists and production assistants for the Scottish Film Industry. A short, intensive, introductory course is followed by a wide variety of attachments to independent productions, usually in Scotland. The number of places is limited and evidence of previous experience and a long-term commitment to the industry is sought. Details are available from:
The Film and Video Technician Training Scheme
Scottish Film Training Trust
74 Victoria Crescent Road
GLASGOW G12 9JN

The Gaelic Television Training Trust

The Gaelic Television Training Trust, jointly run by Common na Gaidhlig, Scottish Television and Grampian Television, offers grants to allow a limited number of Gaelic speakers to undertake a year's on-the-job training in production skills at either of the two television companies so that they can then enter the freelance market.

Evidence of an individual's commitment to work in the industry is essential.

Applications should be made to either of the two television companies or: Chairman, Gaelic Television Training Trust,
Sabhal Mor Ostaig College,
An Teanga,
ISLE OF SKYE IV44 8RQ
Tel: 04714 373

Other Courses

For details of other training courses which may be suitable for those entering the industry or those wishing to develop their careers, please see:

- *Directions* – a guide to practical short courses in film and video.
- *Film and Television Training* – undergraduate and post-graduate courses with a practical emphasis.
- *Studying Film and Television* – courses in higher education which include film and/or television as part of their syllabus. The emphasis is on theory rather than practice.

All the above are available from:
British Film Institute Publications Department,
21 St Stephens Street,
LONDON W1P 1PL
Tel: 071 255 1444

Accessing Film, Television and Video Training in Scotland available from:
Scottish Film Council,
74 Victoria Crescent Road,
GLASGOW G12 9JN
Tel: 041 334 4445
Price £1

Note: The courses mentioned in these publications are not necessarily known to the ITV companies, and no guarantee can be given of their quality.

Distance Learning

BBC Television Training produces a large range of television production videos. These are available only to schools, colleges and training establishments. Details are available from:
BBC Television Training
BBC Elstree Centre,
Clarendon Road,
BOREHAMWOOD,
Herts WD6 1JF

Workhouse Ltd is developing a range of distance learning packages which include videos and supporting written material. The titles which are currently available are 'Research and Scripting' and 'Production Management'. Other titles should be available shortly. Prices are in the region of £600. Details are available from:

The TV Works,
Workhouse Ltd,
Granville House,
St Peter Street,
WINCHESTER,
Hants SO23 9AF

Workhouse Ltd and *19* Magazine have also produced 'The *19* Guide to Careers in Television' (on video).

National Vocational Qualifications

The broadcast, film and video industries are currently developing National Vocational Qualifications (NVQs) for the industry, and the first courses leading to television-related NVQs should be available in 1993.

The Government intends that all industries in the United Kingdom should introduce NVQs as soon as possible in order to increase the relevance of vocational training to the world of work.

The advantages to individuals attending NVQ accredited courses are that:

1 The training is practical and job related.
2 The standards of competence are determined by the industry and measured by the industry.
3 They provide proof for employers of what the trainee is able to do.
4 Certain skills which are common to several industries can be transferred, thus easing the movement of labour from one industry to another.
5 They can be built on throughout a career. NVQs do not only relate to junior entry level but will ultimately extend to all levels in all jobs.
6 The various 'Units of Competence' can be mixed and matched to suit the needs of the individual, thus it may be possible to gain an NVQ to demonstrate a certain level of competence in camera operations and combine that with NVQs in sound, editing, or perhaps management.

7 The training can be delivered in many ways – through colleges, universities, private sector establishments, on-the-job or perhaps in some cases by open learning.

It is likely that the introduction of NVQs to the television, film and video industries will radically alter the provision of pre-entry vocational courses. Many of those listed in this chapter are likely to be modified to comply with the requirements of NVQs.

Some colleges offer City and Guilds 770 as the equivalent of NVQ Level 2. This is an interim measure until the industry has produced its own qualifications.

WORK EXPERIENCE

Many courses of study include a period of work experience as a compulsory part of the programme.

ITV recognises the importance of such experience both to the individual and the industry, and each year several hundred students are given attachments with the ITV companies.

Regrettably, the demand for work experience far outstrips the supply of suitable opportunities for training, and ITV must therefore restrict attachments to those applicants who will gain the most from them. The criteria which are normally applied are as follows:

1 Applicants must be students following a recognised course of study (such as a degree, or BTEC), at a college or university.

and

2 The course which they are following must be vocational, leading to the possibility of employment within the television industry. Ideally, work experience should be a compulsory part of the course.

and

3 The student must be resident in the transmission area of the company offering the attachment, or in some cases, attending a course in that area.

ITV does not normally offer work experience to students who are studying subjects which are unrelated to the work undertaken by a television company. Opportunities may however occasionally exist for students following computing, librarianship, finance, legal, administrative or management courses.

Applications from teachers and lecturers for attachments to their local ITV station may be considered if the courses for which they are responsible are particularly relevant to the television industry.

Applications from school children are not normally accepted owing to the heavy demand for attachments from students, and the lack of opportunities to provide suitable experience.

Work experience attachments may vary in length from half a day to several weeks or months depending upon individual needs and the availability of suitable opportunities for gaining experience.

Students do not normally receive payment from the company. However, students from certain designated courses which are of particular relevance to the industry are paid expenses. Students from sandwich courses who are on long-term attachments may be regarded as short-term employees and paid accordingly.

If you wish to apply for work experience and meet the necessary criteria, you should apply in writing to the Personnel Department at your local ITV company. Vacancies are not normally advertised and are rarely known far in advance. It is never possible to guarantee an attachment, even if you meet the necessary criteria.

TRAINING IN ITV

The section entitled 'Pre-Entry Education and Training Courses' refers mainly to training which is available outside ITV but is relevant to those seeking basic training prior to employment. This section refers to the training that is given by the ITV companies once an offer of employment has been made.

Trainee Schemes

A number of ITV companies occasionally run formal trainee schemes, that is they recruit a small number of people at one time and provide them with a structured programme of training. This is primarily on-the-job but many also include attendance on relevant short courses. The areas in which trainee schemes are usually run are technical operations, journalism, and management although they may be offered in any function if there is a need.

Trainee schemes may not be run every year as they are dependent on the demand for particular skills. They generally begin in September and may last from about six months to two years, depending on what needs to be covered. Some may be open only to women, certain ethnic minority groups or to the disabled where they are under-represented in the workforce.

It is not possible to predict with any certainty where or when trainee schemes will be run.

Young people from different ethnic backgrounds have undertaken a two-year *Jobfit* training scheme at Thames Television. The project develops their skills in camera, sound or videotape operations as the starting point for a career in television. (*Thames TV*)

Graduate Trainees

There are few posts which are open only to graduates, however, there are graduates employed in almost every aspect of television. Applicants of graduate calibre may be preferred for some posts such as management, engineering, design and some areas of Sales and Marketing. Many journalists and researchers are also graduates.

The Editorial Trainee Scheme is aimed primarily, but not exclusively, at graduates and begins in September. Recruitment normally takes place earlier in the year. For further details, see the section on 'Journalists'.

Some companies may offer management or engineering training schemes for graduates from time to time.

Individual Trainees

The majority of trainees who join ITV companies do so as individuals rather than as part of a group. Vacancies may occur at any time of the year in any company and training is primarily on-the-job. It is not possible to predict when vacancies will arise. The company concerned will consider how much experience there is amongst the people already employed and this will help to determine whether or not they can recruit a trainee.

Employment Status of Trainees

Trainees are usually recruited on a contract for the duration of training. There is no guarantee of employment on completion of training but whenever possible a further fixed term contract will be offered on satisfactory completion of training.

Training for Experienced Employees

A wide variety of training courses is available to the employees of ITV companies. These courses may help them to develop their careers, learn new skills or adapt to changing technology. Many of these courses are organised by individual ITV companies for their own staff according to current needs. Some training may be in the form of attachments, for example if employees need to learn more about other areas of the company in order to do their jobs better.

Attachments may also help employees to see if they are fitted for other kinds of work.

Where there is a common need across the network, the ITV Association organises courses to which any of the ITV companies may subscribe. These include courses in production, technical operations, journalism, management and any other aspects of working in television. The courses cover basic training and development training. Current examples include a trainee journalists scheme, stereo sound training, camera operations, a trainee directors course, development skills for women and a number of management courses. The ITV Association does not have its own training facilities but draws on technical resources in the ITV companies and at other centres such as Ravensbourne College. Tutors are highly experienced staff or freelance practitioners.

TRAINING FOR EXPERIENCED FREELANCERS

It is vital for freelancers to keep up to date with changing skills and technology in the industry. Many who are on long-term contracts with ITV companies will be trained in the same way as employees. The ITV companies also provide training specifically for freelancers from time to time.

Courses run by the ITV Association are open to suitably qualified freelancers. They will generally need to meet their own course fees, although an ITV company might pay if it feels it is of benefit to the company to invest in such training.

The National Short Course Programme at the National Film and Television School also provides short courses for freelancers. The fees at the NSCTP are subsidised.

A number of training organisations offer short training courses which are suitable for freelancers as well as employees of companies. These include:

Ravensbourne College of Design and Communication
Tel: 081 468 7071

The Royal Television Society
Tel: 071 387 1332

BKSTS
Tel: 071 242 8400

The Freelance Training Fund has recently been launched by ITV and Channel 4 to try to address some of the problems of funding training for freelancers. Support is given to courses which meet a training need which has been identified by the industry. If for example a shortage of skilled Vision Mixers is identified, some funding will be given to courses which deliver appropriate training at a sufficient level of professionalism. It should be noted that financial support is given to the course organiser to enable fees to be reduced, not to individual freelancers seeking training. The Fund is currently administered by the Training Department at the ITV Association although this arrangement may change in 1992 or 1993. Courses which are supported by the fund are normally advertised in the trade press or other appropriate media. At the time of writing, courses with Freelance Training Fund support were run by the ITV companies, the National Short Course Training Programme and the Scottish Film Council. The number of suppliers is likely to increase in 1992. The Fund also supports the development of Open Learning projects for the training of freelancers in television.

Booklist

General

Working in Television by Jan Leeming. Batsford Academic & Educational Limited

Film & TV: The Way In. A Guide to Careers. British Film Institute

Training and Careers in Film and Television. The Association of Independent Producers

Education, Training & Working in Film, Television & Broadcasting by Dennis Boxall. British Kinematography Sound and Television Society, 549 Victoria House, Victoria Place, LONDON WC1B 4DJ (available only from the publishers)

One Day in the Life of Television, edited by Sean Day-Lewis. Grafton Books

Production Techniques

Directing the Documentary by Michael Rabiger. Focal Press

The Production Assistant in TV and Video by Avril Rowlands. Butterworths/Focal Press

Script Continuity and the Production Secretary by Avril Rowlands. Butterworths/Focal Press

The Technique of Documentary Film Production by W Hugh Baddeley. Butterworths/Focal Press

The Technique of Lighting for Television and Motion Pictures by Gerald Millerson. Butterworths/Focal Press

The Technique of Television Production by Gerald Millerson. Butterworths/Focal Press

On Camera by Harris Watts. BBC Publications

Video Active by Geoff Elliott. BBC Publications

Techniques of 3 Dimensional Make-up by Lee Bagyan. Watson & Guptill (UK Distributor – Phaidon Press)

Stage Make-up by Richard Corsan. Prentice Hall (UK Distributor – IBD Publications)

Television Graphics by Douglas Merritt. Trefoil Design Library

Journalism

The Technique of Television News by Ivor Yorke. Butterworths/ Focal Press

News – Whose Bias? by Martin Harrison. Policy Journals

News, Newspapers & Television by Alastair Hetherington. Macmillan

Engineering/Technical

Colour Television Theory by Hutson. McGraw-Hill

Broadcast Television Fundamentals by Michael Tancook. Sony Broadcast & Communications UK – Pentech Press

Stereo Sound for Television by Rumsey. Butterworths/Focal Press

The Video Studio by Alan Bermingham. Focal Press

Television Sound Operations by Glyn Alkin. Butterworths/Focal Press

The Techniques of a Sound Studio by A Nisbett. Butterworths/Focal Press

Using Video Tape by J F Robinson and P H Beards. Butterworths/ Focal Press

Recording Techniques by Robert Runstein. Howard Sams, (UK Distributor – Pitman Publications)

Basic TV Technology by R L Hartwig. Focal Press

Video Tape Editing by S E Browne. Focal Press

Electronic Post-Production and Video-Tape Editing by A Schneider. Focal Press

The Art of Digital Video by John Watkinson. Focal Press

The Art of Digital Audio by John Watkinson. Focal Press

Colour Television by Hutson. McGraw-Hill

The Reproduction of Colour by Hunt. Fountain

Writing

Screenplay (Foundations of screenwriting. A step by step guide from concept to finished script) by Syd Field. Delacarte Press New York (available from Ian Mead Ltd, UK)

Scripting for Video & Audio Visual by Dwight V Swain. Butter-worths/ Focal Press Media

Writing for the BBC. BBC Publications, 35 Marylebone High Street, LONDON WIM 4AA

A Practical Manual of Screenplaywriting by Lewis Herman. New American Library 1952 (available only from the US or from specialist bookshops)

The Writers' and Artists' Yearbook. A & C Black (annual)

Note

There are many trade magazines which will give you a considerable amount of information about television. Examples are *Broadcast, Marketing Week, Television Week, Campaign* and *Audio Visual.*

Butterworths/Focal Press publish a wide range of books on film television and photography, not all of which are listed here.

BBC Television Training publishes many books on television production. Details can be obtained from BBC Television Training, BBC Elstree Centre, Clarendon Road, BOREHAMWOOD, Herts WD6 1JF.

The national press also carries many informative articles about developments in television, as well as programme reviews.

▌▌ *Places to Visit*

If you would like to find out more about working in the television and film industry, the following are worth a visit:

- Granada Studios Tour, Water Street, Manchester.
- The Museum of the Moving Image, South Bank, London.
- The National Museum of Photography, Film and Television, Prince's View, Bradford.

Many television companies will organise group tours of their studios by special arrangement with their Public Relations Department.

It is also possible to obtain tickets for audience shows from the Public Relations Department of your local ITV company.

HOW A DRAMA PROGRAMME IS PLANNED AND MADE

This diagram shows the various stages in the making of a television programme, in this case a drama. Broadly similar procedures are followed for all other types of programme. Note the emphasis on planning and preparation, and the inter-relationships between the various jobs and departments.

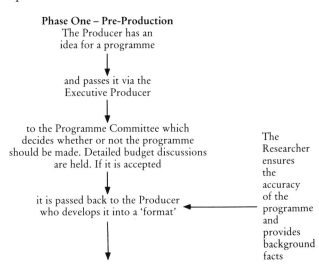

Phase One – Pre-Production
The Producer has an
idea for a programme

↓

and passes it via the
Executive Producer

↓

to the Programme Committee which
decides whether or not the programme
should be made. Detailed budget discussions
are held. If it is accepted

↓

it is passed back to the Producer
who develops it into a 'format'

↓

The Researcher ensures the accuracy of the programme and provides background facts

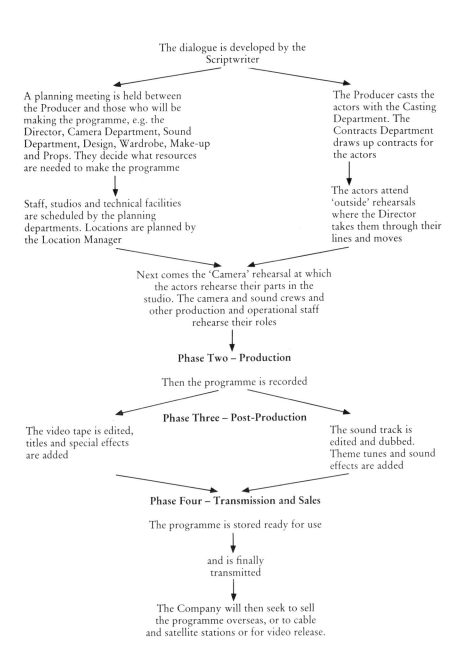

The dialogue is developed by the
Scriptwriter

A planning meeting is held between
the Producer and those who will be
making the programme, e.g. the
Director, Camera Department, Sound
Department, Design, Wardrobe, Make-up
and Props. They decide what resources
are needed to make the programme

The Producer casts the
actors with the Casting
Department. The
Contracts Department
draws up contracts for
the actors

Staff, studios and technical facilities
are scheduled by the planning
departments. Locations are planned by
the Location Manager

The actors attend
'outside' rehearsals
where the Director
takes them through their
lines and moves

Next comes the 'Camera' rehearsal at which
the actors rehearse their parts in the
studio. The camera and sound crews and
other production and operational staff
rehearse their roles

Phase Two – Production

Then the programme is recorded

Phase Three – Post-Production

The video tape is edited,
titles and special effects
are added

The sound track is
edited and dubbed.
Theme tunes and sound
effects are added

Phase Four – Transmission and Sales

The programme is stored ready for use

and is finally
transmitted

The Company will then seek to sell
the programme overseas, or to cable
and satellite stations or for video release.

Overlaps between jobs

The descriptions of jobs which follow have been arranged in alphabetical order for ease of reference. It is important to remember however that there is often a high degree of overlap between jobs and many staff, and to a lesser extent freelancers, are skilled in two or more areas. Some will be highly skilled in one job but will be able to assist in another when called upon to do so. Others, such as news crews, may be equally skilled at camera operations, sound and editing.

The following list shows the main jobs which fall within each functional area of television. Most of the overlaps between jobs will occur within the same function, although there are exceptions. Different companies combine jobs in different ways according to their size and the nature of their operation. This does not mean that job applicants need to have all the qualifications needed to do every job! They should select the job which interests them the most and ensure they meet the requirements for that post. They should, however, expect to be trained in other areas as well, once they have joined the industry.

Function Areas

Programmes:

Casting
Producer
Director*
Researcher
Journalist*
Script Editor
Music Services
Writer

Production:

Camera Operator
Production Manager
Costume/Wardrobe

Props and Stagehand
Director
Set Design
Floor Manager
Sound Technician*
Graphic Designer*
Special Effects*
Lighting Director
Technical Operator*
Location Manager
Make-up Artist
Vision Mixer
Production Assistant

Post Production:

Editor (Film and Video Tape)
Graphic Designer*
Sound Technician*
Special Effects*
Technical Operator*

Technical:

Engineer*
Technical Operator*

Transmission/Presentation:

Engineer*
Programme Planner
Transmission Controller

Front of Camera:

Announcer
Journalist*
Performer
Presenter

Weather Forecaster

* – appears in more than one function.

Some common examples of jobs which are combined are cameras, sound and editing; sound and electrician; lighting and electrician; props/stagehand and rigger-driver; floor, location and production manager; director and vision mixer; and director and producer.

Part Two

JOB AND ENTRY REQUIREMENTS

ADMINISTRATION

When you think of the kinds of people employed in a television station, it is the programme-makers who immediately come to mind. There are, however, many administrative staff employed by the ITV companies and it is undeniable that employment prospects are generally more likely to occur in administrative rather than programme making areas.

The administrative functions of the television station provide an essential managerial and support role for the programme makers. They employ people at all levels from clerks to senior managers.

Some of the main administrative areas are as follows:

The Company Secretariat

Most companies have a Secretariat which is responsible for the legal aspects of running the business. The Company Secretary is a senior manager who may well hold professional accountancy, legal or administrative qualifications.

The department usually employs a small number of staff who look after the needs of the Board of Directors by preparing minutes of meetings and writing reports and papers. They also ensure that statutory records are provided to various government bodies, that legal aspects of the purchase, sale and administration of property are correctly carried out, and they look after the insurance of the company's property and staff. Previous knowledge of television can be helpful, but is not essential.

Accounts

The Accounts function of a televison station falls very broadly into two sections. Firstly there is the section which deals with the finances of the company, frequently known as Financial Accounts.

Staff in this area assist in planning and controlling departmental budgets, providing statutory and internal financial reports, controlling payrolls, etc. Senior members of this section are normally qualified Accountants but administrative staff with an aptitude for figures are also employed.

Secondly there is the Programme Accounts section which is responsible for estimating and monitoring the cost of making programmes. On the whole, the Accountants who are employed in this section have some previous experience in film or television since they may be asked to cost a script with very little assistance from the Director. A knowledge of how programmes are made becomes essential when the Programme Accountant is asked to estimate the likely cost of using a particular location, of buying or making particular props or comparing the cost of making the programme on film, in the studio, or on outside broadcast. In some companies at least, part of this role will be covered by a Production Manager, although that title may cover a variety of different tasks. Programme Accountants are usually qualified Cost Accountants.

Purchasing

This department is responsible for the purchase of office equipment and general materials for the smooth running of the company. Staff employed in this area are responsible for receiving purchase requisitions from departments, for ordering items from suppliers, and for receiving and checking invoices for payment. Industrial purchasing experience is useful for senior posts.

The Purchasing department is not normally concerned with the purchase of items for inclusion in programmes. This is the function of the Production Buyer.

Employee Relations

The Employee Relations Department normally consists of the Personnel, Recruitment, Training, Welfare, Safety and Industrial Relations functions. The title of the department may vary from company to company and certain functions may be grouped together. In general, however, the main duties of the department are very similar to those in any other organisation and include the provision of a recruitment service, the organisation of training, job grading and review, salary administration, the keeping of Personnel records, counselling and advisory services for staff, the implementation of safe working practices, and the provision of specialist advice to line managers on the maintenance of good industrial relations. In some cases the administration of the Pension Fund may also be carried out by the Employee Relations function.

Managers in this area will normally have appropriate professional qualifications such as those awarded by the Institute of Personnel Management (IPM). It is not uncommon for administrative staff in the Employee Relations function to progress into management having obtained professional qualifications.

Contracts

Actors, dancers, musicians and most other people who appear on television are not permanent employees of the ITV Companies, but are contracted on a temporary basis for the duration of a programme or series. It is the responsibility of the Contracts Department to organise the payment of their wages and other conditions of their employment.

Many programmes are repeated and the Contracts Department then arranges for 'residual rights' payments to be made to the various artists who appear. In addition, payments have to be made to musicians whose recorded work has been chosen for use in a programme, perhaps as a theme tune or as incidental background music. Payments are also made to authors whose work is used, for example, as a basis for a drama series.

In some companies, the Contracts Department may be responsible for casting for programmes, although in larger companies, this is generally the responsibility of the Casting Director.

A thorough knowledge of contract law, copyright law, employment law and the negotiated agreements between ITV and Equity, the Musicians' Union, the Writers' Guild, or the various staff unions is essential. Considerable experience in the television industry is required for posts in this department, and/or a legal background.

House Services and Transport

The House Services Department is responsible for the provision of office and other general facilities. Tasks may include the allocation of office space, the planning of future expansion, the organisation of telephone systems and cleaning services, the purchase of office furnishings and the provision of postal and printing services. Jobs may be filled internally or externally and previous experience in television is not essential.

Security Officers may also be employed by the House Services department, although in some companies they are employed on contract. Security staff are responsible for the protection of all the company's premises and equipment, and may typically be former police officers or former employees of major security companies.

The Transport Department is responsible for the smooth operation of the company's vehicles including film crew cars, outside broadcast scanners and an assortment of other vans, lorries and cars. Senior posts are normally filled by applicants with experience in the buying and selling of vehicles in bulk, and an up-to-date knowledge of transport law.

Education and Community Liaison

A small number of people, often with previous teaching experience, are employed to liaise with schools, colleges and local authorities on the use of ITV programmes for educational purposes. They may also carry out general liaison duties with the viewing community, usually in conjunction with the Public Relations Department. In some companies, this department is closely associated with the making of educational programmes and there may be opportunities for Education Officers to be Producers on such programmes. In other companies, the department is more closely aligned to the Public Relations function. Some previous contact with the television industry is desirable.

Production Planning and Scheduling

The Production Planning Department is responsible for the long-range forecasting of the requirement for studio time, equipment and staff in order to meet the company's commitment to make programmes. The Production Scheduling or Production Control Department is responsible for allocating studio time, equipment and staff to each programme and for monitoring progress until the programme is completed.

There is a variety of administrative and managerial jobs in these areas, some of them requiring more experience in television than others. All, however, involve considerable contact with other departments in the company and staff will be expected to develop a thorough knowledge of staff trade union agreements in operation in the company.

Programme Planning

This department is responsible for planning the schedule of programmes to be shown in the local region. There is a considerable amount of liaison with other ITV companies to co-ordinate the transmission of networked programmes, with the Sales department for the scheduling of advertising breaks, and with the Presentation Department for the scheduling of promotions, announcements, etc. Senior posts are normally filled internally, but more junior vacancies may be filled by external applicants with clerical, secretarial or administrative experience.

It is not possible here to give more than a general idea of the kinds of qualifications needed by applicants for administrative posts. More senior positions in the Legal, Personnel and Accounts departments, for example, may demand the appropriate professional qualification. Applicants for middle graded posts will generally have a good record of GCE O level or GCSE passes (grades A to C), including English and Mathematics, and ideally A levels in any subject. Junior posts may be filled by applicants with O level passes and GCSE's (grades A to C). Once again, English and Mathematics are most useful. All posts are likely to demand a high degree of accuracy, attention to detail, and the ability to develop and work to systems. The ability to communicate effectively in writing, on the telephone and face to face, is also important.

See also – 'Librarians', 'Computers', 'Management', 'Secretaries and Clerks'.

ANNOUNCER AND PRESENTER

Announcer

The job of the television Announcer must seem to the public to be one of the most glamorous jobs available, and this is reflected in the overwhelming response received by the television companies whenever such jobs are advertised.

It is certainly true that the job can bring instant public recognition, with offers to make appearances at fêtes and local shows, etc., and all the pleasures and problems that this entails.

There is however much more to the job than meets the eye. Announcers must be prepared to accept very considerable disruption to their private lives as they offer a service to the public which covers 24 hours a day, seven days a week.

The most obvious task undertaken by Announcers is the provision of a link between programmes, introducing the next programme to be screened, and previewing others to be shown later on. Within the industry, they are frequently known as Continuity Announcers, and this reflects their role of ensuring a smooth progression from one item to another.

The job involves a great deal of behind the scenes preparation and Announcers sometimes write their own scripts, although this may be done by Promotion Script Writers. They must therefore be able to write clearly and concisely for the spoken rather than the written word. They must also make sure that they are fully aware of any problems or events that might mean an interruption to normal services. A newsflash, for example, may have to be read in the middle of a programme, and there will be very little time to prepare a script. If there is a technical breakdown, the Announcer must keep the viewers informed and the ability to 'ad lib' can be very useful to fill a gap before normal services are restored.

Other duties may include on-screen interviewing, reading scripted commentaries for various programmes, doing 'voice-overs' on television commercials, reading news bulletins, compering programmes and carrying out research and preparing scripts for programmes.

Announcers also have a very important sales role to play, since the aim of all television companies is to reach the maximum number of viewers. The manner in which Announcers introduce or preview a programme can have a significant effect on whether viewers decide to watch. They must therefore have a broad range of interests and a good general knowledge so that they can introduce all types of programme from soap operas to documentaries with genuine interest and understanding.

Announcers, more than any other staff, represent to the public the image of the television companies for which they work. The programmes may come from any of the ITV companies or an outside production company, but the viewers know that the Announcer is part of their local ITV station. It follows that the different companies may look for very different kinds of Announcer to reflect their own image.

There are, however, certain qualities which all Announcers should possess. They must have poise and presence and be able to speak with an air of authority. They must have a warm, friendly, approachable personality, an attractive appearance and a clear well-modulated voice which is pleasant and easy to listen to. Regional accents are acceptable and, indeed, may help to reflect the local image of the company.

Experience has shown that the best Announcers have often received speech and drama training and preference is given to applicants with experience in the entertainment industry. From time to time applicants without such experience are successful, and trainee vacancies are sometimes offered to people who are totally new to television announcing.

Presenter

Television Presenters are responsible for taking the lead in, or 'fronting', programmes. They are the well-known personalities who are associated with certain news, sport, current affairs programmes, documentaries and quiz shows, etc.

It is of course impossible to describe the particular qualities required by Presenters, or a typical background from which they are recruited. Each will be different, according to the programme on which they are working.

Presenters on news and current affairs programmes will almost certainly have experience in journalism, and many will have progressed from on-screen reporting on regional news magazine programmes. Reporters may indeed move on to become Presenters on a wide variety of programmes.

Presenters on quiz shows and other light entertainment programmes are often experienced actors and actresses, while Sports Presenters are often well known sporting personalities. Childrens' programmes may provide a good starting point for Presenters without previous experience.

Documentaries are frequently presented by an expert on the subject under discussion, rather than someone with a television or theatrical background.

No recruitment profile is given for this job.

Typical Recruitment Profile

Trainee Announcer

	Essential	Desirable
Physical	Clear, well modulated speech. Smart and attractive appearance. Acceptable to all types of people	Speech training
Education	Minimum of GCSE Grade A to C English language	A levels or degree
Experience		Presentation of any kind
Interests	A wide range of interests of all kinds. Knowledge of television programmes. Wide range of reading interests. Public speaking, hospital radio	
Personal Qualities	Warm, outgoing and friendly but authoritative personality. Poise. Able to remain calm and think quickly under pressure	

Note: Remember that it is how you look and sound to the camera that matters – not how you appear and are heard in the flesh. It may be worth investing in a short video of yourself showing what you can do.

CAMERA OPERATOR

The job of the Camera Operator undoubtedly presents to the outsider an impression of glamour and prestige. Both of these it certainly has to a degree, but as with most jobs in television, the work is demanding, with a long period of training. By no means all of a Camera Operator's time is spent on the camera. They have many other duties, many of which are strenuous, sometimes dirty and often uncomfortable.

The majority of programmes seen on television are pre-recorded on video tape from pictures shot on electronic (video) cameras. Electronic cameras are also used for the relatively few 'live' programmes that are shown (mostly news, current affairs and chat shows).

A comparatively small number of programmes are, however, shot on film. The main examples of film on television are some, though not all, commercials, some full-length drama features, both old movies and those produced for television, and some documentary material. Film possesses certain qualities which have in the past been lacking in video tape, however advances in technology have enhanced the quality of video. Since it is generally cheaper and more convenient to use, an increasing number of programmes are being made on tape at the expense of film. This should pose no real dilemma for a young person wishing to start a career in film camera operations, for it is relatively easy for the skills acquired in film to be transferred to electronic cameras.

Nowadays, the word 'film' is used quite haphazardly to describe any television material that is not being transmitted live. One also hears the occasional reference to 'live filming', e.g. of the Cup Final. Such inaccuracy is pardonable since it conveys a concept that is easily understood, however it is highly probable that the programme has been made on tape, not film.

For the sake of clarity, we shall describe here the work of the Camera Operator under four headings: Studio, Outside Broadcast, News and Film.

Studio

A typical studio may have three, four, five or even six electronic cameras in operation at one time, according to the kind of programme that is being made. Most of the cameras currently in operation are fairly large and are positioned on a pedestal, supported on mobile mountings. The mountings glide smoothly over the floor and enable the Camera Operator to position the camera for any kind of shot.

Each camera is operated by one person, but there are other supporting members of the team or 'crew'. Some studio cameras, for example, are mounted at the end of a jib on a motorised crane which can be raised to a considerable height, or lowered to within an inch or two of the floor.

In addition to the Camera Operator who is seated at the end of the jib operating the camera, there may be a second member of the team whose task is to 'swing' the counterbalanced arm. A third member, seated at the back of the crane, is responsible for driving it accurately to precise positions marked on the studio floor. The tasks of driving and swinging the crane are just as much a part of camera work as operating the camera.

Camera Operator using a studio camera at Central Television. (*Central TV*)

Lightweight studio cameras can also be mounted at the end of a long crane arm and operated by remote control by a Camera Operator on the studio floor – a different skill again.

The majority of cameras currently in use in studios have the encumberance of long cables which snake across the floor to sockets in the studio, and via them to the control equipment. These cables have to be constantly man-handled to allow the cameras freedom of movement. This task is known as 'cable bashing'. In some companies, cable bashing is the responsibility of the junior members of the camera crew, while in others everyone takes their turn.

An Electronic Camera Operator working in the studio (or on OBs) generally has less discretion than a Film Camera Operator in how the action will be shot. The Programme Director will normally decide the relative positions of the cameras, and the size of shots. During the camera rehearsals for a recorded programme, the Camera Operator will practise taking up these positions, following a check-list of agreed shots which is attached to the camera. During the recording, the Production Assistant will remind the Camera Operator via the 'talk-back' system of the shots which are coming up.

Although some very experienced Directors will dictate the precise composition of the shots, most will simply call for a 'close-up' or 'two-shot' or whatever and the framing and composition of the shot will be left to the Camera Operator. A skilled Camera Operator will anticipate the kind of shot that the Director is seeking and 'offer' the shot on the studio monitor for selection. This is particularly useful during live shows when there is little chance for rehearsal.

Another of the Camera Operator's skills is the ability to reposition the camera quickly and frequently without causing obstruction to the other cameras, microphone booms, and artists. Excellent hand-eye co-ordination is needed for zooming, etc.

The work can be very tiring as Camera Operators must stand for long periods under hot studio lights. They must also have the personal qualities needed to work as a member of a team. They must be able to help artists to give their best performance since the working relationship between the artist and the Camera Operator is often very close.

Smaller cameras are increasingly being used in the studio, and may be hand-held on the shoulder, or mounted on a pedestal as necessary. In certain cases, such as some news bulletins, the operation and positioning of these cameras may be remotely controlled by computer so that there is no Camera Operator on the studio floor.

▥ *Outside Broadcasts*

The traditional 'OB' unit is a mobile studio control room with a number of cameras linked to it. Such units are mainly used for state occasions, sports fixtures, political conferences, and other events which take place away from the studio.

There are, however, increasing numbers of 'mobile' units which make use of small, lightweight cameras to cover OBs, and to record inserts for dramas and other studio productions. These units may consist of several cameras, or just one portable single camera (PSC) which is used by the Camera Operator in much the same way as a film camera.

Whatever the kind of unit, there are common problems which the Camera Operator working outside the studio must face. These include finding a suitable place to position the camera, which may be on a scaffolding tower, a roof or a grandstand in less than ideal

Camera Operator and crew on location for *About Anglia Xtra*. (*Anglia*)

conditions. The weather can also be a problem and the Camera Operator must be prepared to work in the cold, the wind, and the rain.

News

News camera operations requires a special kind of individual. They must not only be technicians, but both individualists and team players. They are leaders, artists and entrepeneurs who often live on their wits and may have to rely on other members of the news crew for their safety. The 'street-wise' skills of News Camera Operators are often as important as their technical and artistic abilities. News is often unpredictable and Camera Operators cannot know in advance what difficulties and dangers they may be asked to face, or what human emotions they may have to confront. A high degree of fitness and stamina are essential.

It is the responsibility of the Camera Operator to seek out the most telling pictures. An ITN News Camera Operator in Kurdistan. (*ITN*)

There is no Director to decide what shots are to be taken for a news item. It is the responsibility of the Camera Operator to seek out the most telling pictures.

The title of Camera Operator is becoming something of a misnomer in relation to news. They may work in a team of only two, carrying out all the functions of cameras, sound, lighting, simple editing, first-line maintenance of their complex gear, manning electronic communications links equipment, and playing material along lines and satellite links back to base.

In some cases they may work entirely alone, carrying out as many of these functions as are practical at any given time with PSC equipment. In either case, they must use their initiative since they have little of the support that is available in the studio.

Entry into the profession can be via a number of routes. In most regional ITV companies, news is combined with other camera operations such as studio OB and film, and Camera Operators may be rostered onto news for several weeks at a time. At ITN, however, News Camera Operators are specialists. Some may have begun their careers in regional television companies as part of a news crew, or some other technical job. Some are appointed directly from outside if they are able to demonstrate that they are 'naturals' for on-the-road work.

Most ITV companies use the services of 'stringers' from time to time. These are freelance News Camera Operators who cover a particular geographical region and can be quickly on the spot when a story breaks. They may send pictures to one or more company or news organisation.

Film

Film is still used fairly extensively in the television industry as many practitioners believe it can provide a picture quality which is not attainable on video. Many programmes are therefore shot on film and then transferred to video tape for transmission.

Most Film Camera Operators also work with video, though there are still some who specialise exclusively in film.

The top jobs in film cameras are those of the Lighting Camera Operator. They are the senior technicians on film units and are responsible for both the technical and artistic quality of the pictures. With the Director, they make the major decisions about the positioning of cameras, the way in which the action is shot, and how the scene will be lit to meet the needs of the action. In this respect, Film Lighting Camera Operators tend to have more artistic discretion than Electronic Camera Operators. Lighting Camera Operators also supervise the work of the camera crew. On a big 'shoot' where several scenes or locations have to be filmed in sequence, they may well leave the operation of the camera to one of the crew whilst doing the lighting for the next action area.

Lighting Camera Operators tend to be specialists in either documentaries or dramas, and when working on an assignment, will normally be away from base for several weeks, travelling extensively and coping with novel situations.

Exterior Camera Operators are the next rung down the ladder. They do much the same job as Lighting Camera Operators but usually on less prestigious productions, perhaps specialising in documentary work. In some companies, however, the grade of Exterior Camera Operator no longer exists.

Next are the Camera Operators who, normally under the supervision of a Lighting Camera Operator or Lighting Director, work the camera on every kind of shot. They may also work unsupervised as News Camera Operators.

The Camera Assistants, or 'Focus Pullers' or 'Clapper Loaders' are the least experienced of the crew. They are responsible for the care and cleanliness of the camera, loading and unloading film, and keeping records of all 'takes'. On long tracking shots where the camera has to move towards or away from the action, the Camera Assistant operates the focus control on the camera. After starting as a trainee and working for nine months under the supervision of another Assistant, plus about another two years alone, the Camera Assistant will 'act up' as Camera Operator coping with ever more complex shots.

Working on a film unit involves a good deal of travel and long periods spent away from home on locations, often in bad weather. It is not the job for anyone who likes an ordered existence or a comfortable life.

Typical Recruitment Profile

Trainee Camera Operator

	Essential	Desirable
Physical	Stamina and agility. Good colour vision. Able to hear instruction clearly through headphones. Co-ordination of sight, touch, hearing and general movement	A good head for heights
Education and Training	Broad general education to at least GCSE standard (grades A to C)	GCSE grades A to C in English and maths, physics. A levels (subjects not specified). Knowledge of lighting, optics. Film and television or photographic course at college of further education. An understanding of electronics is useful for work away from the studio
Interests	Practical evidence of interest in and flair for photography (preferably cine or video), from artistic and technical point of view	Amateur dramatics, current affairs, TV, films, theatre

	Essential	*Desirable*
Personal Qualities	Equable, sociable temperament. Able to act on own initiative	

COMPUTERS

All of the ITV companies use computers, and most have their own computer departments. The titles of these departments vary, but they may be described as Computer Services, Management Information Services, or Information Technology Services for example. Most such departments are small and employ no more than a handful of people. Some are continuing to grow as new computer systems are introduced.

Mainframe computers have been in use in ITV for many years, often linking the various companies. Others link the Sales Departments (which sell advertising time), with leading advertising agencies.

Minicomputers and small personal computers or PCs have been increasingly used in recent years. They frequently link individuals and departments within the company.

The applications of computers in television are too numerous to mention, but they include:

- Accounting and financial management
- Programme planning and production planning
- Controlling the sales of advertising time
- Personnel records
- The preparation of programme scripts
- Graphic and set design
- Designing new equipment
- Controlling automatic studio equipment such as lighting
- Library records and control
- Word processing
- Newsroom operations

Most engineers employed in ITV need to be able to use computers and to carry out computer programming in engineering computer languages. As new technology advances, the engineers and the specialists from computer departments need to work increasingly together. Computer specialists must keep up to date with the new technology, and must of course learn how a television station operates. They have regular contact with people in all departments where computers are used, and must be able to communicate technical concepts clearly and effectively with non-technical people.

Opportunities for employment may arise at a number of levels. Business Analysts and Systems Analysts may be employed by some companies to investigate organisational and management information problems, and to decide whether computers can offer a solution.

Programmers may be employed to write instructions for the computer to enable it to perform the desired task, while Computer Operators will load and operate the machinery. Specialist Operators may be employed on large systems to type in quantities of information, and distribute printouts.

It is sometimes possible to join as a Trainee or as an Operator and to progress upwards to Programmer, Analyst, or Operations and Systems Manager level. This can however take a number of years and cannot usually be done without studying for professional qualifications. Higher Diploma or Degree qualifications are common at more senior levels, as are qualifications awarded by the British Computer Society.

Typical Recruitment Profile

Computer Operations

	Essential	Desirable
Physical	Good hand-eye co-ordination. Manual dexterity. Capable of learning to touch type	
Education and Training	A level GCE in Computer Studies	BTEC Higher Computer Studies.

	Essential	Desirable
		Knowledge of electronics or physics
	Note: (1) Some Government funded long term training schemes requiring 4–5 good GCE O Levels (or GCSE) may be a substitute. (2) Some companies may accept trainees with lower academic qualifications who are able to pass an aptitude test in logical thinking	GCSE grades A to C physics, English, maths
Personal Qualities	Calm temperament. Able to concentrate on detail	

Typical Recruitment Profile

Trainee Programmer/Analyst

	Essential	Desirable
Physical	As for Trainee Operators	
Education and Training	A level GCE computer studies. Some companies may accept trainees	Degree in computer science and student graduate of British

	Essential	Desirable
	with lower academic qualifications who are able to pass an aptitude test in logical thinking	Computer Society. (Minimum entry 2 A levels)
Personal Qualities	As for Trainee Operators. Plus an analytical problem-solving mind	

▦ Typical Recruitment Profile

Business/Systems Analyst and Operations Management

	Essential	Desirable
Physical	As for Trainee Operators	
Education and Training	Degree in computer sciences, or full membership of British Computer Society, or combined degree in business studies and computing	Second degree of comparable qualifications in business studies if not incorporated in First degree. Four to five years relevant experience and some line management experience
Personal Qualities	Calm temperament. Inquisitive and analytical. Strong interpersonal skills; able to interview 'client colleagues'	

COSTUME DESIGN AND WARDROBE

Independent Television has produced many memorable drama productions in which the magnificent costumes have contributed much to the impact of the programme. Costumes also play a vital part in many light entertainment shows, particularly those that feature dancers. Most of these programmes are, however, made by the larger ITV programme companies or commissioned from major independent production companies. Career opportunities in costume/wardrobe in the smallest companies are limited. The demand for wardrobe facilities is so variable that even the major companies rely heavily on freelance and contract staff when they are making a major programme. There are a number of differences in the job titles used in the various ITV companies and in the content of jobs. For the sake of simplicity, we have used the title of 'Costume Designer' here, but in many companies, similar tasks are carried out by the Senior Wardrobe Supervisor.

The most senior posts are held by Costume Designers. They usually work on the most prestigious programmes and their responsibilities include planning, management of staff, designing, fitting and budgeting.

The planning stage is a vital one, and Costume Designers (or their equivalent) must read the script thoroughly before deciding what type of costumes will be appropriate. The wishes of the Programme Director must of course be taken into account and consultation must take place with the Set Designer to ensure that costumes and sets blend together in perfect harmony. The plans may have to be changed once the casting has been done as the chosen costumes may not suit the artiste.

Costume Designers must plan the entire operation down to the last detail including when changes of costume are going to be necessary. They may design costumes which are to be made up from scratch, or plan alterations to transform existing costumes or accessories.

It is of course impractical for television companies to carry large stocks of clothes and most costumes are hired from theatrical costumiers. Costume Designers visit the costumiers with the artistes to select and fit suitable clothes. They may also supply the accessories and trimmings that will help to transform the clothes to reflect the right period or the right character. Any alterations that are needed to the clothes at this stage are usually done by the staff at the costumiers.

The job clearly calls for a high degree of creativity combined with administrative and supervisory skills, the ability to interpret written ideas, and the ability to work well with artistes. They must also be prepared to spend long periods researching to ensure that costumes are authentic. They must possess a thorough knowledge of fabrics and costume styles appropriate to various periods. A thorough understanding of dressmaking techniques is also essential. If the production is very large, they may be assisted by a Wardrobe Supervisor or an Assistant who will help with the fittings and the general running about. These staff carry out many of the same duties as the Costume Designer, except designing, and are responsible for wardrobe continuity. They often work on shows which require modern dress and are therefore frequently called upon to take artistes shopping for clothes.

Below the Wardrobe Supervisor is the Wardrobe Assistant/Dresser. One of the main functions of the Dresser is to help artistes into and out of their costumes during the production and to have ready any changes of clothes that may be necessary. This part of the job calls for tact and discretion as many artistes are under considerable stress before a performance. Dressers must have the ability to sense how artistes wish to be treated. Some will enjoy a chat while they are being dressed, while others will prefer a courteous silence. It is important that Dressers are confident, but not over-confident, and not too familiar.

This same sensitivity to other people is of course an essential qualification for every grade in the Costume and Wardrobe Department.

Dressers also carry out minor alterations to costumes, sometimes at the very last minute, and the ability to sew quickly and neatly is therefore important. They are also responsible for the general care of clothes and accessories including washing, cleaning and pressing.

Since Dressers do not design clothes or carry out major alterations, they do not require tailoring or design training. If they wish to move up the promotion ladder, such qualifications will become increasingly important.

All grades of staff may be called upon to work in the Studio and on location. Unsocial hours are common, and location work frequently means working under difficult conditions.

Typical Recruitment Profile

Wardrobe Assistant/Dresser

	Essential	Desirable
Physical	Normal colour vision. Hand to eye co-ordination. Clean, neat and tidy. Good personal hygiene	
Education and Training		GCSEs (grades A to C) in English, history, art, mathematics, dressmaking
Experience		Employment in theatre or film Wardrobe, or with a theatrical costumier
Interests		Creative fashion. Art, television, theatre, history
Personal Qualities	Tactful and discreet. Sensitive to the needs of others. Sociable, practical	

Note: Applicants who wish to progress to more senior grades, particularly Costume Design, should preferably have attended an Art College course in fashion or theatre design, or an apprenticeship in tailoring. Creativity and artistic ability is essential for senior posts together with an excellent sense of fashion.

CRAFTS AND TRADES

There are a number of crafts and trades within Independent Television. Some of the staff are employed solely on site maintenance and some are specialist craft workers who apply their skills to television production. Those employed on site maintenance cover the normal range of duties associated with their trade.

Not all ITV companies employ people in these grades. Some contract out the work to specialist organisations.

Carpenters and Joiners

Carpenters are employed in the general installation and maintenance of all wooden items in offices and other premises.

Building a set in the Construction Shop at Central Television. (*Central TV*)

Others are employed in the construction of sets for television programmes and may be called upon to make an endless variety of items from antique furniture to the interior of a spaceship. Most of the sets are dismantled after use, so there is little point in using all the skills of the craftsman to make them last. Some items, such as chairs, however, must be able to stand a fair amount of wear and tear and must be made to the highest standards. Carpenters work from drawings made by the Set Designer and the ability to interpret drawings accurately is most important as it is in all crafts.

Painters

Painters are employed for the painting and decorating of offices and other premises.

Others are employed to paint the sets for television programmes and they are called upon to use a variety of skills not normally required of a painter and decorator. They may paint 'walls', 'doors' and 'floors', etc., under the guidance of the Set Designer.

There is scope for considerable creativity when, for example, they are asked to turn a plain piece of wood into an 'antique door', or reproduce an elaborate 'plaster moulding' that will withstand the close scrutiny of the camera.

Drapes/Upholstery

Some of the larger companies employ upholsterers to make soft furnishings for studio sets. They follow detailed plans prepared by the Set Designer to make such things as curtains, or padded upholstery for the interior of a 'pub'. Only small numbers of staff are employed in this field.

Plumbers

Plumbers are of course employed to carry out the normal range of plumbing duties on the company premises and may maintain heating and ventilating systems, etc. They are also required to provide plumbing facilities for studio sets. They may, for example, be responsible for supplying water to the taps in the sink on a set depicting a kitchen.

Fitters/Mechanical Maintenance Engineers

These staff are responsible for the maintenance of any mechanical equipment on the premises including camera dollies, microphone booms, film editing machines, etc.

Electricians

Electricians are employed by the ITV companies in a variety of jobs associated with the installation and maintenance of electrical facilities and the lighting of studios for programmes.

The task of the House Electrician is to install and maintain lighting and power supplies, etc., in offices and other company premises, and to supply power and light to studios and technical areas.

Production (or Lighting) Electricians on the other hand are employed to set up lamps in the studios. A typical television studio has lighting grids in the roof from which a variety of shapes and sizes of lamps are suspended. It is the job of Lighting Directors to plan how the lamps should be arranged to create the desired effect for a particular programme. The Production Electricians use these plans to move the lamps along the grids and into the correct position. They are also responsible for ensuring that the lamps are fully operational. A good head for heights is needed for this job! Production Electricians are also employed in a similar function on outside broadcasts and film locations although in these cases the lamps are usually free-standing or fixed to scaffolding or anything else that happens to be available.

In some companies the job of House Electrician and Production

Electrician are totally separate but in others they are combined. Electricians may be recruited as House Electricians, Production Electricians or both, and where the jobs are separate, staff may sometimes move from one to the other after a period of time.

All Production Electricians must be prepared to work irregular hours and House Electricians must work shifts. All are on call now and again at irregular times. Production Electricians are also required to work away from home, sometimes under difficult conditions with a minimum of supporting facilities.

Recruitment

Staff may be recruited into these posts as qualified craftsmen and tradesmen* or, from time to time, traineeships may be available. Companies prefer to recruit craft trainees locally and vacancies are normally advertised through local careers offices, Job Centres and local newspapers.

The traineeships or apprenticeships last for three or four years and combine periods at college on day or block release with practical on-the-job training. Applicants are expected to have a good standard of education and entry qualifications are usually related to the further education course to be followed by the apprentice. GCSE grades A to C in English and Mathematics are both useful.

Although applicants for traineeships are most likely to be 16 or 17 years of age, favourable consideration will be given to older applicants who have been made redundant from apprenticeships in similar fields in other industries.

No recruitment profile is given for these posts, but applicants for all jobs must be prepared to work irregular hours or shift work. They must also be prepared to travel away from base on occasions.

In some companies staff have ceased to specialise in one craft or trade, and have become multi-skilled across a range of jobs.

Note: These terms apply equally to men and women.

Typical Recruitment Profile

Craft Trainee

	Essential	*Desirable*
Physical	Normal colour vision. Good hand-eye co-ordination	16–17 (unless redundant from another scheme)
Education and Training	Should have studied to GCSE standard in at least four subjects including maths, English, and either physics or technical drawing (especially Electrical Trainees)	
Interests		Electronics (for Electrical Trainee)
Personal Qualities	Able to use initiative and to work as a member of a team. Willing to undertake further study	

DIRECTOR

A television programme of any kind invariably starts life as a collection of ideas, probably embodied in a script. The Programme Director's job is to take those ideas (to which he/she may well have already contributed) and to translate them into the sequence of pictures and sound ultimately seen by the viewer.

The translation requires the skills of a great many people. It is the

Director who plans and controls the activities of those people and to a large degree it is the Director's skill at motivating them to give their best that determines the excellence of the finished programme. In order to do this successfully the Director needs a thorough appreciation of everybody's job and the technical or artistic limits within which they are constrained to work. For instance, the ITC sets high technical standards for the quality of the pictures and sound in a programme. If the Director wants to create a particular visual 'mood' effect such as the warm glow of a fire in a darkened room, the production team can easily produce it. But the actors will not experience that mood easily because even the darkest parts of the set will need to be quite brightly lit in order to achieve the correct technical balance. An experienced Director will know this and will plan accordingly.

At its most sophisticated level the job of the Director is to create say, a television drama, shot by shot, coaxing the utmost from actors, and the production team. When shooting is complete, there follows a long period of post-production editing and sound dubbing which the Director must supervise.

At a more basic level, for instance on a news magazine programme, the Director follows a running order of items, selecting pictures from the shots offered by the camera operators and relaying 'speed-up', 'slow-down' instructions to the presenters.

Both these examples present their own challenge: the first, that of achieving artistic excellence; the second, that of converting chaos into order. Both also demand a high degree of leadership and the ability to get on with all types of people.

Clearly there are Directors and Directors. Not all are equipped to work on a prestige network drama. By mid-career most Directors will have found their level and/or their forte. Drama is not the only area that calls for special directorial skills. Light entertainment, sport and music are all areas where reputations can be made. Every company needs a number of competent generalist Directors who, though they may not be truly gifted, can turn out a good programme in any area. Many companies require Directors to have equal facility with both video and film production although, as video cameras get smaller and lighter, the differences of technique between film and video are diminishing rapidly.

Some Directors are also Producers, but the combination of the two roles can make heavy demands on their time.

There is no clear-cut path leading to the job of Director. A very small number of theatre Directors make the transition to television by direct entry. In the main though, trainee Director posts are filled from within the industry by people with substantial experience of production. Traditionally the most popular sources of directorial talent have been Floor Managers, Camera Operators and Researchers, but this list is by no means exclusive. Just about any job in television production can be the stepping-off point for a career in direction. Some companies now combine the job of directing local news with other production posts and this can provide staff with an opportunity to discover a talent for directing.

The competition for trainee posts is intense in the extreme. For those who make it to the top, the rewards in terms of job satisfaction are substantial.

Trainee Programme Director

No recruitment profile is given for this job, as it is impossible to describe a 'typical' Director. Candidates will in general be already employed in television, in jobs described in other sections of this book.

EDITOR: FILM AND VIDEO TAPE

Editors are currently employed in two areas – film and video tape, although the number employed exclusively in film is very small. In most ITV companies the jobs have been combined into one role, sometimes called a 'Picture Editor'. Most Editors can expect to work on programmes produced by electronic 'Portable Single Cameras' (PSC), also known as 'ENG' or 'EFP' (Electronic News Gathering or Electronic Field Production) according to the type and scale of production.

The Editor's work begins when most of the rest of the production team has finished and moved on to another production. The Editor's task is to assemble the constituent parts of the programme, remove the pieces that are not needed, and present the programme in its final form ready for transmission. The sound department may be required to carry out some work on the sound track after editing has been completed but, in essence, it is the Editor who is responsible for creating the final form and style of the programme. Editing is therefore an essential function in all programmes, except those which are totally live or recorded continuously and require no 'post-production' work.

Film Editing

The fundamental difference between editing film and editing video tape is that film is physically cut and video tape is not. Film usually requires a great deal of editing as programmes are frequently shot on one camera only. This leads to a considerable amount of out-of-sequence shooting. The types of programmes which are sometimes made on film are documentaries, and dramas made on location.

The Editor views the developed film frame by frame with the Programme Director and decides where cuts should be made. 'Takes' that were unsuccessful are removed, scenes are arranged in the correct order, and individual frames may be removed to create a better effect. The sound track is also cut to coincide with the picture. Once the cuts have been made, the film is re-assembled using transparent joining tape or a special cement to produce the 'cutting-copy'. The job clearly calls for a high degree of precision and artistic flair and meticulous attention to detail. Editors must be familiar with the technicalities of film processing and materials so that they can pass instructions to the film laboratories who will produce the final copy.

It takes a long time to build up the knowledge and experience needed to be a skilled Film Editor, and most begin their careers as Trainee Assistant Film Editors, moving on to become Assistant Film Editors.

Assistant Film Editors do not make editing decisions, but provide the support services needed by the Editor. Their main task is to synchronise the 'rushes'. The picture and sound tracks are separated and the original picture negative is stored away safely to keep it in

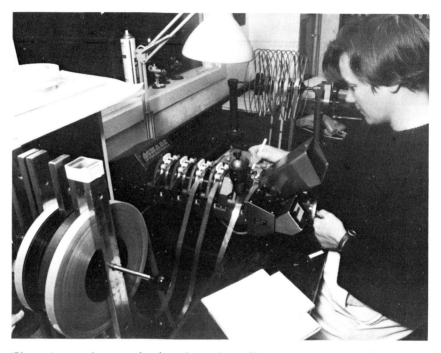

'Pic-sync' – marrying a soundtrack to pictures in an editing suite at Cosgrove Hall Productions (Thames Television's animation subsidiary). (*Thames TV*)

prime condition until it is time for the final editing to be done. The Assistant Film Editor lines up a copy of the picture 'takes' with the sound tracks by co-ordinating the picture and sound of the clapper board. It is then ready for the Editor to work on. Other important duties are looking after the equipment in the cutting room, cutting and joining film, and keeping thorough records. There may be hundreds of strips of film in the cutting room, some waiting to be joined together and some waiting to be discarded. The Assistant Editor makes a note of what is on each strip, and the editing decisions that have been made. All discarded film is carefully logged and stored away so that it can be quickly located if the Editor suddenly decides to use it. Very neat handwriting, attention to detail, and an orderly mind are essential qualifications for the job.

Promotion to Film Editor is not automatic and will depend on ability and the availability of posts. It may take several years, but most experienced Assistant Film Editors will be given practical experience of minor editing tasks to help them to compete for promotion.

Video Tape Editing

The majority of television programmes are made on video tape. There is therefore a heavy demand for video tape editing. The equipment used by a Film Editor is relatively simple and hand operated. Video Editing machines on the other hand are sophisticated pieces of electronic equipment and this explains why many present Video Tape Editors began their careers as television engineers and technicians. It is not essential however for a Video Tape Editor to have a technical background. The operation of the machine can be learned in a relatively short time and it is the ability to make the right editing decision that is important. Once the Editor and Programme Director have decided where the edit points should be, the scenes to be retained are recorded onto another tape, the original remaining untouched.

A video editing suite at ITN. (*ITN*)

Video Tape Editors may come from a variety of backgrounds but all will have some previous experience in television.

The role of the Assistant (or Junior VT Engineer/Editor) in video tape editing is similar to that of the Assistant Film Editor but with some important differences. The Assistant is responsible for 'lining-up' the machine, i.e. setting up the controls ready for use, and the general fetching and carrying of tapes, etc. It follows that a technical background is desirable for an Assistant and entry is often through the Technical Operator route. Promotion to Video Tape Editor is possible for those with the necessary qualities. Not all companies employ staff in the Assistant grade.

Editing Single Video Camera Production – PSC Editing (ENG & EFP)

Any Editor will work under extreme pressure from time to time, but it is particularly true of the ENG Editor working on a news programme. Most of the items will have been recorded that day, and the Editor has very little time to view the tapes, identify the key elements of the stories in conjunction with the Reporters, and assemble news items of exactly the right length and content before the programme goes out.

A few ENG Editors, mainly at ITN, are expected to carry out maintenance on their equipment since for reasons of efficiency they sometimes work 'in the field' rather than at base, and consequently do not have engineering support.

EFP production is used for location work in drama and light entertainment. Many 'Film' Editors now train in EFP.

The skills needed by an Editor working on film or tape, are somewhat difficult to define. A knowledge of television production techniques is essential as the Editor must know which shots will cut together and which will not. For example, two shots of the same moving car taken from either side will not cut together, as it will appear to the viewer as if the car is suddenly changing direction.

A degree of creativity is also essential since a cut which is made a few frames too early or too late can greatly diminish the aesthetic effect of a scene. In addition, creativity must be combined with ingenuity on the occasions when there seems to be no way that two shots can be cut together!

The ability to listen to other members of the team such as the Programme Director, and understand and interpret their ideas is important, together with the ability to put one's own ideas into words.

An interest in current affairs and a broad general knowledge is a great advantage since in the course of their careers, Editors will work on a wide range of programmes. An understanding of the subject matter can be of great assistance in creating the right atmosphere in a programme.

Editors are usually assigned to a programme or series, so that they have the satisfaction of following a job right through. They frequently work alone although several Editors may work on a very big production.

Editing is of course a long-term career in itself and with increased experience an Editor can hope to progress to ever more demanding programmes.

Applicants from outside the television industry who do not have previous experience can enter the editing field directly by applying for posts as Trainee Assistant Film or Film/ENG Editors. All other editing posts require some relevant experience in television, e.g. as a Vision Mixer, Engineer or Technical Operator.

Typical Recruitment Profile

Trainee Assistant Editor

	Essential	Desirable
Physical	Good colour vision. Good hand-eye co-ordination	
Education and Training	Broad general education to at least GCSE (grades A to C) standard.	GCSE English (grades A to C). Adequate numeracy
Experience		Knowledge of film stocks and processing.

	Essential	*Desirable*
		Knowledge of video tape production
Interests	Any aspect of photography or film making. An interest in all kinds of television programmes.	
Personal Qualities	Attention to detail. Observant. Able to work under pressure. Innovative. Creative	

ELECTRONIC ENGINEER

Television is a medium which relies for its existence on the skills of the Electronics Engineer. Many of the areas in which Engineers are employed are described in the section on Technical Operators, but in addition Engineers are employed in the following.

■ *Planning/Installation/Research and Development*

This section is responsible for the detailed planning of new technical projects to provide the facilities required by the operational staff. The work requires expertise outside traditional electronics skills, since there is a need to understand the difficulties and limitations imposed by building and air conditioning requirements. An understanding of project management and budgeting is also essential.

Once the planning is completed the section is responsible for carrying out the installation. If outside contractors are used, the section will supervise their work. Considerable time is spent on acceptance tests of new equipment and systems, a duty which is often shared with engineers from the maintenance department.

In addition to planning and installation, this section is often heavily involved in the assessment of new equipment or systems prior to purchase decision being made.

In some of the smaller companies this function is incorporated within the maintenance department.

Maintenance Department

All studio centres have an electronic maintenance workshop where repairs and routine servicing of equipment is carried out.

Advances in micro-technology have resulted in more complex equipment with built-in automatic correction circuits, minimising the need to recruit operational staff with a technical background.

As a result, operational engineers in some companies are now only responsible for first line maintenance, with the maintenance depart-

Maintaining broadcast machinery at Grampian Television. (*Grampian*)

ment of specialist engineers undertaking the major technical work-load.

In addition to the routine maintenance and repair of broadcast equipment, such as electronic newsgathering cameras, computer graphics, video tape recorders, edit controllers, etc., some maintenance sections undertake a varied amount of development and design work as well as evaluation and acceptance testing of equipment prior to purchase.

Typical Recruitment Profile

Trainee Engineer – Maintenance

	Essential	*Desirable*
Physical	Normal colour vision. Good hand-eye co-ordination	
Education	(1) BTEC Higher Certificate Diploma in Electronics with TV or communications, or (2) City & Guilds T5, or (3) HNC/HND in engineering or electronics or telecommunications	Degree in engineering or electronics or telecommunications
Interests	Electronic and non-specific wide range of technical team-work and media related interests	Ability to demonstrate practical aptitude

Typical Recruitment Profile

Trainee Engineer:- Planning, Research, Installation and Development

	Essential	Desirable
Physical	Normal colour vision. Good hand-eye co-ordination	
Education	Degree in engineering or electronics telecommunications. (Applicants wishing to follow a career in projects will be expected to gain initial experience in other engineering departments)	(1) Honours degree in engineering or electronics or telecommunications (2) Project management awareness (3) Financial management awareness (4) Technical report writing ability
Interests	Electronic projects and a wide range of technical, teamwork and media related interests	

FLOOR MANAGER

Including Floor Assistant and Stage Manager

The responsibilities of the Floor Manager fall into two main areas: (1) liaison between the Programme Director and the studio floor and (2) management of the studio floor.

It is of course the Programme Director who has overall responsibility for how a programme is made. During studio rehearsals and the final recording however, the Director is seated in a control room which is usually separated from the studios by a glass screen, and views the proceedings on a bank of television monitors. The Floor Manager receives instructions from the Director via headphones and

Floor managers are the co-ordinators and managers of all that is happening on the studio floor. A studio in action at Anglia Television. (*Anglia TV*)

takes action accordingly. The Director may for example decide during studio rehearsals that an actor should move to another position, or speak his lines in a different manner. It is the Floor Manager's responsibility to pass on these instructions in a way that will achieve results. This often demands a great understanding of human nature, since the actor may already be under considerable pressure, or may have different ideas from the Director about how the part should be played. Similarly, Floor Managers may have to coax nervous members of the public into talking on local magazine programmes. They also give performance cues to the performers and provide prompting where necessary.

Floor Managers will work with many different Directors over a period of time and should be able to understand the way each one likes to work and anticipate their wishes.

Floor Managers are also the co-ordinators and managers of all that is happening on the studio floor. They not only make sure that artistes are ready when needed, and that any extras and walk-on artistes know where to stand and what to do, but also ensure that all the other aspects of the production are ready when required. Props must be in position, cameras and microphone booms must be correctly positioned according to the plans, make-up must be completed on time and a host of other items must be checked. Once again, this aspect of the job demands considerable interpersonal skill since the members of the production team are all experts in their own fields. It is important that Floor Managers are able to command the respect of the production team even though they may not have the technical knowledge that the team members have.

If there is an invited audience, the Floor Manager is responsible for their safety, well being, and involvement in the programme.

The amount of responsibility that Floor Managers are given depends upon the Director, and varies between companies. Some may be given the task of deciding the order in which scenes are to be shot. Some may also be responsible for drawing up the final script (i.e. the total plan of action for sound, cameras, artistes, etc.). In many companies however, these tasks are not carried out by the Floor Manager.

The Floor Manager is present at outside rehearsals (which are held mainly for drama and some light entertainment productions). These are the early rehearsals which are usually held in large public halls away from the studio. The Floor Manager is mainly a bystander at this stage, taking the opportunity to learn the production very thoroughly, and making constructive suggestions to the Director about how things could be improved.

Floor Managers also work on outside broadcasts, carrying out much the same function as in the studio.

In many companies, Floor Managers are also involved with film production in the capacity of Assistant Directors. The responsibilities and techniques are different from those in video tape production. First Assistant Directors have wide authority in many areas. In the pre-production period the First Assistant will work with the Production Manager to 'break-down' the shooting script and examine the likely requirements and responsibilities. The 'First' will also work closely with the Director to find out what he/she has in mind and how the whole film is visualised, and will then develop a very detailed shooting schedule. Additionally, it is the 'First's' responsibility to co-ordinate any special effects, stunts, and casting, etc. An awareness of Health and Safety in the working environment is essential, including knowledge of the relevant legislation.

The job is very demanding both physically and mentally. The Floor Manager must have a total understanding of the production, and complete commitment to it. At the same time, the job calls for long, irregular working hours, and very little opportunity to sit down for a rest. An equable temperament is necessary to cope with the crises that may occur, particularly on programmes which are live rather than recorded. It is easy to see that academic qualifications are less important for the job than the right personality and plenty of enthusiasm.

In the past many Floor Managers have started their careers as Floor Assistants, which is the equivalent of a Runner (or 3rd or 4th assistant) in the film industry. Floor Assistants are an essential part of the production team, particularly if a large drama is in production, however very few are now employed in ITV. Their role is to make sure that performers are in the right place at the right time, and that they are made comfortable at all times.

Today Trainee Floor Managers may be recruited from a wide variety of jobs in the television industry and many learn the basic skills during a period of secondment from another section such as cameras, production assistants, etc. They are rarely recruited from outside unless they have similar experience in the theatre. Junior staff usually assist more experienced Floor Managers, and may work on their own on short, straight-forward programmes.

Stage Manager

The role of the Stage Manager is to organise outside rehearsals including the arranging of rehearsal rooms, ordering and moving of rehearsal props, keeping the script up-to-date during rehearsals, prompting the performers, ensuring continuity of props, marking out the floor of the rehearsal room, etc. They are mainly employed on dramas.

All Stage Managers have extensive experience in television or the theatre. This is a job which is fast disappearing as the duties are absorbed into other jobs such as Studio or Floor Management.

Typical Recruitment Profile

Trainee Floor Manager

	Essential	Desirable
Physical	Good stamina, agility. Able to hear clearly over headphones. Clear speech	
Education and Training	Broad general education to at least GCSE (grades A to C) standard	GCSE (grades A to C) in a range of subjects
Experience	Experience of handling large groups of people in stressful situations	Experience of working with actors in theatre, film or TV. General experience of the business including technical aspects of television
Interests	Drama	Music. Any aspect of film, television and theatre

	Essential	*Desirable*
Personal Qualities	Confident and genial personality. Able to understand and handle all types of people. Sense of humour. Self-discipline and initiative. Unflappable. Tactful. Sensitive to performance. Leadership	

GRAPHIC DESIGNER

Graphic Designers are normally employed within the Design Department and usually work alongside the Set Designers. Their work is most frequently seen in the opening and closing titles of a programme, but they can be called upon to undertake a host of other tasks including the preparation of cartoon sequences, weather charts, economic forecast charts and even such things as old bank notes, letters, driving licences, paintings, etc., for use as props in drama programmes. The range of tasks is endless and the job calls for considerable ingenuity and imagination.

The simplest opening titles consist of the name of the programme superimposed on the first scene. More complex opening titles might include moving cartoon sequences or photographs and once again the Graphic Designer is responsible for preparing the constituent parts. The wishes of the Programme Director must of course be taken into account, as must the wishes of the Set Designer and other members of the production team. There must be continuity of theme and mood between graphics and sets, and both must reflect the atmosphere of the programme if they are to be effective.

Most of the work of the Graphic Designer is done on computers. Computer graphic systems such as 'Paintbox' enable the Graphic Designer to experiment in ways which are not possible using the more traditional methods. Suppose for example that the Graphic Designer 'paints' a picture of a girl in an apple orchard, but is then unhappy with the colour and layout. The colour of the apples or anything else, can be changed instantly and the girl can be moved from her original position to another point in the picture to produce the desired effect.

One area of graphics which is not normally the responsibility of the Graphic Designer is the production of captions showing, for example, the name of someone being interviewed for a news item or a sports programme. These captions are produced by the Caption Generator Operator using a machine similar to a word processor.

The job of the Graphic Designer calls for a wide range of skills, and excellent drawing ability combined with a high degree of creativity is obviously essential. The most sophisticated computer cannot make up for a lack of skill in these areas. The ability to communicate ideas and to be sensitive to the ideas of others is also essential. A wide range of interests and an enquiring mind are very useful as the Graphic Designer can be called upon to work on any kind of programme.

Newcomers will usually begin by assisting more experienced staff on simple graphics. As they develop experience themselves, they will assume increasing responsibility for more prestigious and complex productions.

Typical Recruitment Profile

Trainee Graphic Designer

	Essential	Desirable
Physical	Good colour vision. Able to do fine, detailed work. Good hand-eye ordination	
Education and Training	Degree in graphic design or Licentiate	Some training in fine art

	Essential	*Desirable*
	of Society of Industrial Designers	
Experience		Commercial art studio. Knowledge of photographic techniques. Computer Operation
Interests	Painting/drawing/ graphics. Contemporary design	Photography or other creative hobbies. Theatre film, television
Personal Qualities	Innovative. Ability to communicate ideas. Highly creative	

JOURNALIST

▓ *Including Reporters/Correspondents/News Readers/Editors/Writers*

The term 'journalist' is applied to a number of different grades of staff all requiring a journalistic background.

Journalists are employed both by Independent Television News (ITN) and the ITV programme companies on news programmes. Other Journalists may work on documentaries or current affairs programmes, and some are employed to prepare stories for ITV's teletext system.

ITN has the responsibility for providing the national and international news coverage to the ITV network. It also provides the news on Channel Four and many other bulletins and news programmes.

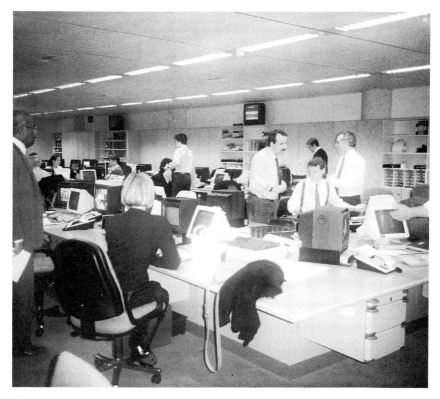

The *News at Ten* desk of the newsroom at ITN. (*ITN*)

The extent of its operations means that ITN employs almost as many Journalists as the rest of the network put together.

Journalists in the ITV programme companies provide regional news and magazine programmes for their own regions. Sometimes they feed regional stories into ITN, but generally ITN sends its own staff to cover assignments throughout the country. Journalists in the programme companies have considerable variation in their jobs, sometimes reporting, otherwise working as Production Journalists in the newsroom.

Any Journalist who works in television news must expect to operate under considerable pressure. News programmes, unlike most others, are live and there are, therefore, strict deadlines to be met. There is also very little preparation time, since news is only of interest if it is fresh.

Newly appointed Journalists at ITN can expect to spend most of their time behind the scenes, searching for stories and writing news scripts. In the programme companies, newcomers may be sent on reporting assignments early on, particularly if the Journalist has broadcasting experience but there will still be plenty of backroom work to do. Promotion to senior posts in both cases is on merit.

Sources of News

Potential stories come from a wide variety of sources. All of the programme companies have extensive local contacts in their own areas, such as local politicians, police, etc., and it is of course important that Journalists are able to develop a good relationship with such people. They also rely on 'stringers', who are freelance Journalists, based in a particular area who feed stories to several news organisations at once. Some stories may be followed up from newspaper or magazine cuttings, and many are 'diary' stories, i.e. they are known in advance, such as sports meetings, royal visits, etc. Many regional companies operate satellite news centres in major towns and cities.

There are several news agencies to which companies may subscribe. Some programme companies take Press Association services for domestic news. ITN subscribes to several news agencies and relies quite heavily on the wire services they provide, especially for overseas news. ITN of course has its own contacts and stringers in the same way as the programme companies and also has its own specialist correspondents to provide news stories.

Visnews is a major independent news organisation which is contracted by at least one company to provide a news service for its regional news and current affairs output. Visnews employs Journalists and news crews and has a world-wide operation.

Reporters

Once the Editor (or in the case of ITN, the Duty News Editor) has decided which news items should be followed up, a Reporter may be despatched to cover the story. If, for example, there is a strike at a local factory, the Reporter will go to the scene with a newscrew to operate the camera, record the sound, and to light the scene if necessary. The Reporter's task is to assess the situation on the spot, decide on the best way to present the story, interview key people such as the Manager and Shop Steward and perhaps prepare a piece in which the Reporter talks directly to the camera, telling the viewer the

A news crew in action for Central Television. (*Central TV*)

background to the story. This is usually done out of sequence, and so notes must be kept to enable the Video Tape Editor (not to be confused with the Editor of the programme) to assemble the item in the correct order for viewing. Reporters must be able to work on their own initiative as there is no Programme Director present to tell them what shots to take, or Scriptwriter to tell them what to say. They must have the social skills to win the confidence of people ranging from old-age pensioners to film stars and politicians. They must be able to formulate the right questions and commentaries on the spot, in a language that will appeal to the most educated and uneducated members of the community.

They must also be prepared for frustrations, as what appears to be a good story can be cut from the programme at the last minute if a bigger story comes along. Since news is a highly perishable commodity the Reporter's work is often in vain as an item can rarely be used in a later programme.

Correspondents

At ITN, and some of the larger programme companies, there are a few specialist Reporters who cover subjects which need an in-depth knowledge. There are, for example, Political, European Diplomatic, Industrial, Crime, Science and Arts Correspondents. Foreign Correspondents for ITN may be based in cities such as Washington and Moscow where there is sufficient news to justify a permanent presence. They become familiar with the local way of life and are accepted by the local community. They send back regular reports, and also report on any major news items that occur in their area. Most of the programme companies do not employ Correspondents.

News Readers/News Presenters/Newscasters

News Readers and Presenters tend to be the personalities of television news. They are usually experienced Journalists. They present news items from the studio and act as anchor men and women, linking and introducing items from various Reporters. Their own scripts may be prepared for them by other Journalists, or they may write their own. They must do a great deal of preparation in a very short time before the programme, making sure they are thoroughly familiar with all the planned news items.

They must also be aware of any developments which mean that last minute changes may be made. News programmes are of course live, and News Readers must therefore be able to cope with any eventuality in a calm, professional manner. They are selected on the basis of their experience in television, appearance, speech and personality.

Working Behind the Scenes

There are a number of other jobs in television news which are carried out by Journalists but which are not visible to the general public.

Scriptwriters for example, are concerned with writing news stories. Their other responsibilities usually include liaising with reporters and technical and production staff on the editing of videotape; organisation of maps, electronic graphics and captions, and scripting the final item to be transmitted.

Editors may be involved in a variety of tasks. In the programme companies for example, the Programme Editor or Executive Editor has the key managerial role for the local news programme. The job usually includes such things as making the final decision on content, vetting items for accuracy, libel, etc., as well as all aspects of planning, budget control, preparation, scheduling management of staff, and ensuring that all deadlines are met. In a small regional company, one person may be responsible for all of these tasks whereas in larger companies there is a hierarchy of staff, including News Editor, Production Editor and Bulletin Editor amongst whom the tasks are divided. In broad terms, the title 'Editor' is given to staff whose job contributes to the overall assembly and preparation of the news programme.

At ITN there are a number of staff involved in the editorial process including Programme Editor, Chief Sub-Editor, Senior News Editors, Duty News Editors, Deputy News Editors, etc. All of these are quite senior positions and are only reached after several years' experience.

Other Posts for Journalists

Journalists are employed as Promotion Scriptwriters, and their task is to produce programme trailers and to prepare scripts for the Continuity Announcers who appear between the programmes.

Typical Recruitment Profile

Trainee Journalist (Programme Companies)

	Essential	Desirable
Physical	Good stamina. Good, clear speech. Appearance which is likely to be acceptable to all types of people	
Education and Training	Two good A level passes, preferably including English	Degree, preferably in English, or a subject related to communications, but the choice of

	Essential	*Desirable* subject is not critical
Experience	About two years' experience in press or radio journalism	
Interests	Current affairs. A wide-ranging taste in reading. Writing. All aspects of the media. Social interests	
Personal Qualities	Self-confidence, leadership, drive, maturity, attractive personality. Able to make quick decisions. Highly articulate, able to remain calm under pressure, enquiring mind, self-reliant, a good command of written and spoken English. Able to win the confidence of all types of people	

Note: From time to time some of the programme companies run formal training schemes for Trainee Journalists without previous experience in the press or radio. These schemes normally begin in September but they are not run every year as much will depend on the Company's staffing needs. They are usually advertised in the national press. Competition for vacancies is very tough.

Journalists (ITN)

Most Journalists at ITN are recruited from the programme companies where they will be expected to have gained a good grounding in television news.

In most years there is a very small intake of graduates for the Graduate Editorial Trainee Scheme. Applicants are normally expected to have a good class of degree and to be able to demonstrate a natural flair for writing news. Previous professional experience in journalism is not essential. The personal qualities mentioned above are equally applicable to candidates for this scheme. Competition for the posts is very tough.

LIBRARIAN

The ITV companies have differing approaches to library services and a variety of job opportunities exists within the industry. Some companies employ Librarians in a general capacity to deal with a number of information sources. Others divide their library service into separate sections such as reference, film and videotape, news information, stills and music with perhaps a library manager in overall charge. Whilst each of these roles calls for certain specialist skills, they all demand at least some understanding of the techniques of television production and an awareness of the deadlines to which programme makers are forced to work.

Most Librarians within ITV are employed in film and videotape libraries handling a variety of broadcast materials for which a level of technical understanding is required. Professional library qualifications are essential in some companies together with some study of non-book materials as part of the course. As the use of computer systems expands, Librarians in the television industry increasingly need to be computer literate. They also need to decide whether to develop library systems within their own companies or to access external commercial databases.

As libraries develop within television, the librarian's role is expanding. They are no longer merely the custodians of various cans of films and cases of video and audio tape but must be able to exploit the information held on the material. ITV library staff are increasingly able to contribute creatively to programme making by informing Researchers, Journalists and Directors of what material is available to them, what music might be suitable and advising them how to successfully exploit the collection. If a request cannot be fulfilled within the company, Librarians should be able to point the enquirer in the right direction, either within the ITV network or the industry generally. After a relatively late start in some ITV companies, libraries are now rapidly developing new systems of cataloguing and classification to cope with information handling in an expanding and changing industry.

The television industry is becoming aware that much of its output has a value beyond fulfilling day to day transmission requirements and, as a result, some companies employ archivists either as part of the library structure or in a separate post to review library holdings and ensure that stock shots and other material of archive importance is permanently retained. Archive material can be of considerable commercial value to a company and is often sold to cable and satellite stations, news organisations, academic institutions and other customers. Archivists and Librarians are often involved in discussing with potential clients what is required. It may be a complete programme or perhaps a standard sequence of a street scene or an aircraft taking off for inclusion in another programme.

Library staff should be capable of working under pressure to meet transmission deadlines. Accuracy of work is also necessary as librarians play an integral role in making sure the correct material is available for editing and transmission.

Those seeking employment in the industry should not have any illusions that the job is a quiet backwater. Life can become pretty hectic when transmission deadlines approach, particularly in the news environment. The advantage of this, however, is that there is rarely a dull moment and the job can be very rewarding compared with more conventional library work.

Typical Recruitment Profile

Trainèe Assistant Librarian

	Essential	Desirable
Education and Training	Broad general education usually	Degree or post graduate diploma

	Essential	*Desirable*
	to degree standard.	in librarianship preferably with non-book materials option.
Experience		Some experience of a broadcast industry library perhaps on placement as part of a degree course.
Interests	Broad, including current affairs, television production and film making. An interest in all kinds of music is essential for music librarians	
Personal Qualities	Outgoing, able to operate calmly under pressure to meet production deadlines. Capable of dealing tactfully and efficiently with a variety of people both face to face and over the telephone. Able to make a creative contribution to programme making. Methodical, attentive to detail	

LIGHTING DIRECTOR

In order to understand the role of the Lighting Director, it is important to appreciate the difference between illumination and lighting. Illumination gives the basic light necessary for the camera to record the picture. Lighting adds to the quality of the picture and can play a large part in creating the right sense of mood and atmosphere. It is also used to add to the illusion that, for example, a television studio is really a living room in a suburban house. Carefully planned lights can make the viewer feel that daylight is streaming in through a window or a front door. The possibilities for the creative use of light are endless and the job can be highly satisfying, even if it is largely taken for granted by the viewer.

Newly appointed Lighting Directors (usually called Lighting Assistants) are allocated to programmes which require fairly straightforward lighting and their work is supervised by experienced Lighting Directors. A news programme for example, is relatively simple to light as the news presenter remains seated and is usually seen against a single, fairly simple background. The task for the Lighting Director is to give the face shape in the most flattering way, and to separate the News Reader from the background, thereby creating a three dimensional feeling to the picture. The technique is very similar to that used by a portrait photographer.

At the other end of the scale, a Shakespearean drama, for example, will present many challenges. Not only are the characters moving around, making it difficult to light their faces perfectly, but lighting has also to be used to create the feeling of dark castles, light streaming from behind pillars, long corridors, and candle light. Clearly, the Lighting Director must work very closely with the Set Designer since poor lighting can ruin the effect of a well designed set.

All members of the production team wili meet early on to plan the production and discuss any conflicting interests. This discussion will enable the Lighting Director to decide how to light the production in a way which will avoid, for example, the lights casting a shadow of the sound boom across the picture.

Electricians then set to work, positioning the lights in the studio in accordance with a chart prepared by the Lighting Director, and under his/her supervision. During the recording of the programme, the brilliance of the lights can be altered as planned from a lighting console in the studio control room. This is done by the Lighting

Console Operator who is an Electrician.

Most of the lights in the studio are fixed to a grid, high in the ceiling, and can be moved around with ease. If the Lighting Director is working on location however, there are many additional problems to be faced. Natural daylight is not particularly suitable for television, and although in programmes such as football matches there is little alternative, a better quality of light is needed for drama and light entertainment, etc. The Lighting Director must therefore have a supply of cumbersome lamps to transport to the location. If a scene is to be shot inside a house, for example, it can be very difficult to place the lamps in the ideal position and the Lighting Director has to resort to ingenuity even more than usual.

Some television programmes which are made away from the studio are on film rather than video, and in these cases, it is the Lighting Cameraman rather than the Lighting Director who is responsible for lighting. The Lighting Cameraman is the most senior member of the film camera crew.

Lighting Directors are recruited from a variety of sources and it is difficult to define a typical career path. They are usually recruited from within the industry and are only recruited from outside if they already have similar professional experience in film or theatre lighting.

The job requires a mixture of technical knowledge and creativity and for this reason, many Lighting Directors have previously worked on camera crews. Some have been engineers and a few have been electricians, but almost any related jobs in television could be a starting point. The technical aspects of the job are mainly concerned with the physics of light and electricity. A high degree of perception, imagination and creativity is also needed.

Typical Recruitment Profile

Trainee Lighting Director (Lighting Assistant)

	Essential	Desirable
Physical	Good colour vision	
Education and Training	Broad general education to at least GCSE grade	GCSE grades A to C physics, maths, art.

	Essential	*Desirable*
	A to C standard.	A levels (subjects not specified).
Experience	Several years' experience in a related department in television	
Interests	Creative, artistic interests	Photography or film making, art and design. Theatre, television and films.
Personal Qualities	Ability to communicate ideas. Creative. Able to supervise staff from other disciplines	

LOCATION MANAGER

It is the task of the Location Manager to seek out and investigate suitable locations for use in the shooting of programmes and, most notably, dramas.

The starting point for the search is of course the script, and the Location Manager will discuss with the Producer and Director the kind of location which will most closely meet their interpretation of the script.

Although it is important to find, for example, a house of the correct historical period or a landscape with the right atmosphere for the drama, there are many other factors which must also be taken into consideration. Ease of access and parking for support vehicles, catering vehicles, crew cars, artists' cars and vehicles needed in the action must be considered. Any inconvenience that is likely to be caused to the owners or users of the property must be anticipated, and steps taken to minimise any disruption.

External factors must also be taken into account, for example noise from aircraft at nearby airfields or traffic on motorways. Even the tidal rise and fall on a river estuary can have an important influence on its use as a location as the continuity of shots taken out of sequence, or over a period of time, will have to be borne in mind.

It is the Location Manager's responsibility to control any factors which can be controlled, and where necessary to negotiate with the Police, local authorities, military authorities, etc., to stop traffic and limit flying, and so on, while shooting takes place. Any factors which cannot be controlled must be taken into account when planning the shooting schedule.

The Location Manager may take a series of photographs to illustrate the proposed locations, and they will be discussed by the production team. If the locations appear suitable, the production team will visit them to ensure that all their varying needs are met.

Once the locations have been chosen, the Location Manger is usually responsible for all the preparatory administration and paper-work. This may include, for example, discussing terms and condi-tions and contracts with land-owners for the use of their property. The contracts will then be drawn up by the Contracts Department. There will be many letters to write, confirming various arrangements with local authorities, etc., and with location caterers who supply meals to the crew and artists during the shoot and during 'clear-up'. In some companies, much of the paperwork may be done by the Production Assistant rather than the Location Manager.

Location Managers must have a sound business sense and the ability to negotiate effectively with officials and members of the public. An ability to get on well with all types of people is essential, together with a thorough knowledge of the requirements of program-me production. Location Managers must be perceptive, have enquir-ing minds, and be able to interpret the Director's ideas when finding suitable locations. Vacancies are normally filled from within the organisation, or by applicants with similar experience in the film or video industries.

No recruitment profile is given for this job.

Make-up Artist

The television viewer is likely to be aware of the work of the Make-up Artist only when watching a drama in which, for example, a character ages over a number of episodes, or a light entertainment

A Make-up Artist at work. (*Central TV*)

show in which exotic fantasy make-up is used for dancers. In such cases as these, make-up is used to transform the performer, either in order to develop a character, or to add glamour.

Much of the work of the Make-up Artist is however 'corrective'. This involves the neatening of hair, the application of powder to shiny noses and foreheads to prevent reflections from the studio lights, and the general tidying of the appearance of a person who is about to appear in front of the camera. Corrective make-up forms by far the greatest part of the job for Make-up Artists who are employed in the smaller television companies. The programmes produced by such companies are mainly news and current affairs, or perhaps quiz programmes in which transformation of appearance is not necessary.

Programmes such as period dramas, science fiction series and light entertainment can present many challenges to Make-up Artists. They may be called upon not only to apply facial make-up but also body make-up for dancers, and to style hairpieces and moustaches, etc.

Experienced Make-up Artists may occasionally work with latex foam or other materials to change the shape of a face, or they may be required to create all kinds of scars and realistic wounds. Such special effects take time, ingenuity, imagination and skill to achieve. Programme Directors decide what general effect is called for, but Make-up Artists must be able to interpret their ideas. They must also liaise with Set Designers, the Costume Department and the Lighting Director to ensure that continuity of style is maintained.

There is of course a much less glamorous side to the job. All members of the Department are responsible for the care and cleanliness of their own equipment, and the cleaning of wigs and other hairpieces is a tedious task. General attention to skin care is also important.

Hairdressing is a major part of the job, and Make-up Artists are frequently called upon to neaten hair, apply heated rollers and wash hair. They should also be able to cut and tint hair in period and modern styles. In many companies, the styling of wigs is an important aspect of the job. Every make-up department will therefore prefer to recruit trainees who have been previously trained in hairdressing.

The job can be very demanding both physically and mentally. The Make-up Artist spends most of the day standing and bending over to apply make-up. This can cause considerable strain to the back and feet. The work is often carried out to a tight time schedule, and during recording or filming the Make-up Artist must be on-hand to touch up or alter make-up as necessary. If the programme is being made on location rather than in the studio, the job can involve standing around in the cold and wet and working without much in the way of back-up facilities.

It is essential that the Make-up Artist has the personality and the maturity to deal with all types of people. Many actors, actresses, politicians and members of the public are nervous before appearing in front of the camera. The Make-up Artist is often the last person they meet before making their appearance, and becomes the focus of their tension.

Entry into the job of Make-up Artist is usually as a trainee. Junior members of staff will normally work as a member of a team on a particular production, under the leadership of a Senior Make-up Artist or a Supervisor. They will gradually take on more responsibility and perhaps work alone on fairly straightforward programmes.

After four or five years' experience, a Make-up Artist may take on full responsibility for a major production as well as supervision of teams of staff. Experienced staff also become involved in research for programmes, such as discovering what type of make-up is appropriate to reflect a given period, or how a bullet wound might look.

Typical Recruitment Profile

Trainee Make-up Artist

	Essential	*Desirable*
Physical	Good stamina. Able to stand for long periods. Personal cleanliness. Normal colour vision. Hand-eye co-ordination	
Education and Training	City & Guilds, BTEC or other recognised qualification in make-up and/or hairdressing, and/ or beauty therapy *or* art school training in portraiture, sculpture or fine art	GCSE (grades A to C) in English, history and art
Experience		Working with people. Experience of theatrical make-up on amateur or professional basis. Experience as a hairdresser or beautician.

	Essential	*Desirable*
Interests	Creative activities, people. Fashion	Television, drama, film, history.
Personal Qualities	Equable temperament, tactful, discreet, creative, artistic, good fashion sense	

MANAGEMENT

The role of Managers in television is in most cases very similar to their role in any other industry. The practice of management begins with supervisors, who although not holding the title of manager, are responsible for the first-line management of staff and other resources. At the middle-management level are Heads of Departments and at senior management level are Controllers, General Managers and Directors including the Managing Director and Chief Executive. This is a rough guide and the number of levels of management varies according to the size of the company.

Some Managers are responsible for the work of large numbers of people while others, particularly those in specialist advisory areas, may have few or no people reporting to them. They are, however, responsible for managing other resources such as time, money and equipment, and for achieving results through others.

There are a number of ways of becoming a Manager in an ITV company. Many of the departments are unique to the industry, particularly those involved in the making of programmes. Most Managers in these departments have worked their way up from the bottom, since it is a great advantage for them to have a thorough knowledge of how television programmes are made. Others may have gained similar experience in another television company and moved across as opportunities occurred.

Examples of management posts which are unique to the industry are the Executive Producer of a programme and the Managing Editor of a news bulletin. Heads of Department and Controllers of production, operational and most technical areas will typically have begun their careers in television.

Some Managers are recruited from outside the television industry. A few may be appointed to manage a department concerned with programme-making, but most are appointed in areas such as Computing, Legal, Personnel, Training, Accounting or Administration. These functions are found in most organisations and consequently there is considerable movement between industries. Such managers usually have the appropriate professional qualification for the area in which they work.

A few Managers are recruited from time to time as trainees by individual ITV companies. They may be given a broad training in a variety of departments in order to gain an overall understanding of the business, and then they may specialise in a particular area. There are no regular intakes of management trainees, and the numbers recruited are very small. Most companies will advertise in the press when they have vacancies. Successful candidates may typically have a degree or professional management qualification, plus a short period of experience in another industry. There are, however, occasional opportunities for internal applicants from any area, to apply for posts as trainee Managers.

There is no recruitment profile given here of the post of Manager, since there is no one background or qualification which is essential. Professional management qualifications such as an MBA (Master of Business Administration), and DMS (Diploma in Management Studies) are becoming increasingly recognised as important in an industry as competitive and commercial as television. The key requirements are the ability to plan, organise, motivate staff and control resources.

Training for new Managers is tailored according to their needs, and may include formal off-the-job training to acquaint them with the industry, or provide them with specific management skills.

Management in television offers variety and challenge in a demanding environment, and the prospect of a first class career.

PERFORMERS

Actors, dancers, musicians and stunt performers are always employed on contracts for fixed terms. There is no such thing as a performer on the staff of a television company. Even those engaged on long running series or serials will be contracted for periods which will rarely exceed 12 months, although there may be options to extend the initial period. The employment of performers is the responsibility of the Casting Department rather than the Personnel Department.

Actors and Dancers

The majority of Actors (and other performers) regard television as one of the media in which they expect to work, and their experience will include acting on the stage, in films, and on radio. The job is allegedly glamorous and for this reason there are always far more people available to act and dance than opportunities for doing so. It is estimated that at least two-thirds of actors are unemployed at any one time. Usually Actors and Dancers will have had previous professional experience outside television before they are employed on television programmes.

There are a number of dance and drama schools throughout the country which offer training, however, they are of varying standards. The best will give a thorough training in performance. It is also possible to achieve training through experience in a repertory company, but this is becoming more difficult with the gradual decline of the repertory movement.

It is sometimes believed that one way to obtain experience as an Actor is by working as a 'walk-on'. This is a performer who is not required to give an individual characterisation, but usually forms part of a crowd scene. It is doubtful whether this work offers any real opportunity to the aspiring actor.

Most Actors and Dancers obtain work by signing a contract with a theatrical agent. A good agent will actively seek the right kind of work for the individual performer, and will have extensive contacts and experience in television, film and the theatre. When performers are required for a television programme, the Producer or Casting Director may approach someone they have seen in another production and feel is appropriate for the part. They may also approach agents to recommend suitable people, and search through casting directories such as *Spotlight*.

Musicians

The great majority of Musicians are casually employed for a particular programme or series. They are usually engaged for a recording session or performance for periods of about three hours. Some companies employ a Head of Music and a Musical Director on the staff. They are responsible for contracting composers, arrangers, and musicians and are always highly experienced. They must have a wide musical knowledge and be capable of advising Producers on all matters concerning the musical content of a programme, whether it is pop music or a symphony orchestra.

Stunt Performers

Stunt Performers are regularly called upon to double for actors, and to act in their own right. Employment as a Stunt Performer in television is normally restricted to those with appropriate experience in the Industry. There is a Register of Stunt Performers. Equity will provide more details of this.

Certain qualifications are recommended. There are a number of categories of stunt and there are appropriate qualifications for each. The 'Fighting' category, for example, includes qualifications in fencing, judo, other martial arts, wrestling and boxing. The 'Falling' category includes qualifications in trampolining, diving and parachuting, while the Agility and Strength category includes qualifications in gymnastics, weight training and ballet and athletic dance.

The world of acting, dancing and making music is highly competitive and there are many hurdles to be overcome. It is, however, a highly rewarding career for those with talent who are fortunate enough to be in the right place at the right time.

PRESS OFFICER

Press Officers or Publicity Officers are employed as part of the Public Relations function. Their main role is to promote the image of the television company and its programmes, and they are responsible for producing high-quality press releases and promotional material. They are used to working under pressure, often to tight deadlines and are able to handle probing questions from the Press, Radio and Television, 24 hours a day, without jeopardising the company's image.

Preparing programme promotional material in the Press Office at London Weekend Television. (*LWT*)

Prior to the launch of a programme or series, a Press Officer will collate a press pack containing photographs, biographies of the performers/presenters together with a synopsis of the programme. They will invite representatives from the media to any promotions held and generally handle any queries or concerns about the programme.

In addition to initiating publicity about the company's programmes, they assist the Press Office with the overall promotion of the company. They are the public face of the company and have to respond positively and immediately to any press release concerning the company or its output.

Typical Recruitment Profile

Press Officer

	Essential	*Desirable*
Education and Training	Two good A level passes, preferably including English	Degree, preferably in English or communications. Journalism course.
Experience	Some journalistic experience. Knowledge of ITV programmes and the ITV Network	Press Assistant experience. Previous television experience.
Interests	Wide ranging taste in reading; writing; all aspects of the media	
Personal Qualities	Proven writing ability, diplomatic responsive/sharp/ decisive, calm under pressure, resourceful	

PRODUCER

Many people do not realise that the role of the Producer is different from that of the Director. Of those who do, a good many would be hard pressed to explain what the differences are. This is not surprising. Often in television the same person wears both hats and assumes the title Producer/Director.

So where does the Producer fit into the scheme of things?

The Producer heads up the Production team that comes together to make a programme or a series of programmes. If you think of a television programme as being like a manufactured product, it is the Producer's responsibility to ensure that the Production team produces the goods on time, at the budgeted price and quality. To do this, the Producer calls on a wide range of specialist and service departments who will advise on how best to carry out the various stages of the production process. Some of this advice will be conflicting and there will also be uncontrollable extraneous factors to take into account. In the end the vital decisions are the Producer's alone. There is a budget to work to, and the Producer must decide how best to spend the money to achieve the objectives in terms of delivery time, quality and price. On larger productions, much of the day to day responsibility for these organisational and administrative arrangements may be passed to the Production Manager or Commercial Manager.

Usually the Producer will be either the originator of the idea on which the programme is based or will have made a substantial contribution to the development of that idea. Sometimes, Producers are lobbied with ideas so it is their job to select from a number of programme possibilities. The Producer will arrange meetings of the production team or meet with individuals to discuss the development and realisation of the idea and then recruit or commission any Scriptwriters.

In television it is the rule rather than the exception for the Producer to make a significant creative contribution to the production. The actual shooting of the programme and the direction of the performers and technical crews are the Director's responsibility. The Producer may, however, take a hand in selecting the Actors or in choosing the locations for a play, and will certainly try to pick the best people for the production team. Ultimately, it is the Producer's responsibility to ensure that people and objects are where they should be, when they should be, for the shoot.

At all times, the Producer's desk is where the buck stops. If bad weather delays outdoor shooting, or the leading actor falls ill, or even (as actually happened with one major ITV drama series) the studio and all the scenery are destroyed by fire, the Producer still has to get the programme made on time. Only in very exceptional circumstances is an over-spend on the programme budget allowed.

We have tended to take as our example someone working in drama, but in fact every programme needs a Producer, who must possess experience and skills appropriate to the type of programme being made. Thus, to succeed in producing light entertainment, a sure instinct for popular appeal and an eye for new talent are essential. In current affairs, sound political and editorial judgement are paramount whilst in sport the skills of commercial negotiation are almost as important as knowledge of the subject matter. Producers generally are intelligent, articulate people with a high level of social and administrative skills.

As with the Director's job, there is no typical career path leading to the job of Producer. Many are ex-Directors or ex-Researchers but just about any job which requires a comprehensive understanding of production techniques can equip you for promotion to Producer.

PRODUCTION ASSISTANT

The job of the Production Assistant is changing like most jobs in television as new technology removes the need for certain tasks to be carried out manually, and simplifies others. The changes which are occurring vary from company to company and depend very much on the type of programme being made. The duties described here, however, give a broad idea of the range of tasks that may be carried out.

Production Assistants are an essential part of the production team and provide both the organisational and secretarial services for the Programme Director. They are in essence the Director's personal assistant and are generally assigned to a particular programme from the start to the finish. Some may move on to another programme before the first is completed. In some companies, mainly the large ones, Production Assistants may specialise in a particular type of programme, such as sport. More experienced Production Assistants may specialise in drama. In many companies, however, Production Assistants work on all types of programme produced by that company, and all will have their share of live programmes, such as local news, at some time.

The Programme Director's office is the focal point to which everyone refers during the making of the programme, and it is the Production Assistant's responsibility to co-ordinate all the various activities.

During the planning stage of a recorded programme, Production Assistants accompany the Programme Director to the many meetings with the production team (design, sound, cameras, lighting, etc.), and with the artists. They make copious notes of all decisions and make

A Production Assistant (left) sits with the Programme Director and Vision Mixer in a control room at Anglia Television. (*Anglia TV*)

sure that the required action is taken. This inevitably involves a considerable amount of routine office work such as word processing, booking rehearsal rooms, technical equipment, hotels, catering facilities, etc.

Next comes the rehearsal period and, since time spent in the studio is very expensive, most rehearsals are held outside the studios. During rehearsals for a drama series or a situation comedy, for example, the Programme Director may decide to change the script and other details several times. The Production Assistant must note any changes, and type and retype the script until the Programme Director is happy. This work is often done under pressure, so fast and accurate typing skills are essential.

The final 'camera' rehearsal takes place in the studio and is a final run through for all the artists and the production team. From this point through to the end of the programme, Production Assistants sit alongside the Programme Director in the control room. One of their roles is to call out instructions to the Camera Operators via the talkback system so that each of them is reminded when they will be 'on air'. Another critical function is to keep an accurate check on the timing of each part of the programme since it will usually be recorded out of sequence.

A stop-watch is used to ensure that the finished programme will be exactly the right length. At the same time Production Assistants must make notes of any further decisions taken by the Director, so they must be able to cope with several tasks at once. The ability to concentrate and think quickly is essential and this is not an easy task at the end of a long day's work in a somewhat claustrophobic control room which has no daylight.

On completion of recording, most programmes require some 'post production' work, i.e. editing and the addition of further sound tracks. If the technicians working on these jobs require any information, it is to the Production Assistant that they turn. The Picture Editor in particular relies heavily on the notes supplied by the Production Assistant.

Some productions may involve assignments on location and, once again, the Production Assistant will keep accurate notes of the proceedings. These may include continuity notes to ensure that the visual flow from one scene to the next is correct. A high degree of perception is needed for this task.

So far, we have referred mainly to recorded programmes, but Production Assistants also spend a significant amount of time working on live programmes in the studio, such as local news. This is particularly so in the first year or two of a Production Assistant's career. Rehearsals for a local news programme are restricted to a quick run-through of the various items about an hour before transmission, and there is no post-production work to be done. The duties of the Production Assistant in the control room are very similar whether the programme is live or recorded. The main difference is that with live programmes there is no room for error and the situation can therefore be very stressful at times. Since local news programmes tend to follow a set format, a good Production Assistant will soon learn to anticipate any problems that might arise, and take appropriate action.

The work is demanding and often means working under pressure in inconvenient and uncomfortable circumstances. Taking notes on location when your fingers are frozen and you are wrapped in several layers of woollens is not easy!

Production Assistants must be able to relate to all types of people in the course of their work, including performers, VIPs, members of the public, and other members of the production team. Some of these people will be nervous or under pressure, and may not be in a co-operative frame of mind.

Recruitment to the post of Production Assistant is usually at Trainee level. Competition for posts is very tough and vacancies are often filled by staff already working for the television companies. Many of these are secretaries and some are in administrative posts. The demands of the job mean that the standard of applicants in terms of personal qualities and educational qualifications must be high.

The work is, however, rewarding and with increased experience, Production Assistants may go on to work on even more prestigious and difficult programmes. This is a job which, more than almost any other, provides an all-round knowledge of the world of television.

Typical Recruitment Profile

Trainee Production Assistant

	Essential	Desirable
Education and Training	Broad general education to GCSE (grade A to C) standard. Subjects to include English. Fast, accurate typing (about 40 wpm) and shorthand (about 100 wpm) or speed-writing. General secretarial skills	A levels (subjects not important).
Experience		Previous secretarial experience and/or experience of organising. A working knowledge of

	Essential	Desirable
		computers or word processors.
Interests	Varied interests including television, current affairs, etc.	Films, theatre, music. Ability to read music.
Personal Qualities	Ability to work accurately and calmly under pressure, assess priorities, organise and think quickly in an emergency. Sensitivity, tact and confidence in dealing with contacts inside and outside the company. Good powers of observation, and an aptitude for mental arithmetic. Able to listen to and interpret instructions accurately	

PRODUCTION MANAGER

Production Associate, Associate Producer

As the title suggests, the role of the Production Manager is to manage the production. Production Managers are not employed by every company or on every production. Their presence is needed most when a long-running series is being made on location. The shoot can last for many weeks or months and careful planning and co-ordination is vital.

The Production Manager joins the production team in the very early days, not long after the Producer. There may not even be a script at this stage. The degree to which the Producer gets involved in the management of the production will vary, but typically the Producer may concentrate on the script and casting, etc. The more practical planning of the production will be left to the Production Manager.

There are as many different ways of doing the job as there are Production Managers, but all will need to work closely with specialists in the production team. There will need to be discussions with the camera section, for example, to determine what equipment is needed and for how long. There may be discussions with the design team, or with the costume department to determine how long it will take for costumes to be prepared and how much they will cost. All of this information will help the Prodcution Manager to plan how much time needs to be allowed for pre-production, production and post-production and to estimate the budget. Tact and diplomacy are clearly needed for the specialists will naturally be wanting to achieve the best results possible while the Production Manager will be only too aware of pressures on the budget.

Responsibility for the budget forms a significant part of the job, and the Production Manager will normally work closely with the Production Accountant. The Accountant brings financial expertise to the discussions while the Production Manager brings an extensive knowledge of the production process.

The Production Manager will normally 'break-down' the script to decide on the shooting schedule. This is the plan of the order in which scenes will be shot, where they will be shot, how long it will take, etc.

Once shooting begins the Production Manager's role is to keep the production on schedule and within budget. This involves sorting out any problems that arise. If, for example, bad weather prevents the shooting of a scene, the shooting schedule must be revised to cause the minimum disruption. This can be difficult if the lead actor's contract cannot be extended because of other work commitments. Technical problems or a host of other unforeseen difficulties might also disrupt the schedule.

The Production Manager will usually be responsible for approving any additional costs that were not foreseen, such as the hiring of additional equipment, provided of course that the budget will allow it. Health and Safety is another important part of the job. The Production Manager is responsible for ensuring that all working practices, from stunts to the positioning of camera, are safe.

By the time the programme goes into post-production, the Production Manager's role is virtually finished although there may be paperwork and other loose ends to clear.

A thorough knowledge of television production is essential for the job and many Production Managers have previously been Floor Managers, Camera Operators, Production Assistants, etc. Some see the job of Production Manager as a rung on the ladder towards becoming a Producer.

Management skills are also essential, for example planning, budgeting and controlling. The human aspects of management are equally important. The ability to lead people by influence and persuasion is vital to the success of the job.

Typical Recruitment Profile

Production Manager

	Essential	Desirable
Experience	Several years' experience in television, film or theatre production	Management of people and resources.
Personal Qualities	Leadership, communication skills, planning, attention to detail, able to respond quickly to changing circumstances, decision making, artistic appreciation, technical appreciation, numeracy	

RESEARCHER

The job of a Programme Researcher in television is a much more broadly based and demanding job than the title suggests. It has few parallels with the kind of academic research familiar to undergraduates. The majority of Researchers work in the area of current affairs programming where their job is journalistic, similar in many ways to that of a Newspaper Reporter. Every ITV company has its own evening news-magazine programme. This is where most young Researchers cut their teeth. They are expected to contribute ideas for the programme and, once the format is decided, to prepare the material for a particular item. This will include identifying and interviewing contacts, obtaining appropriate film or videotape material (usually by going out with a small team to record, but sometimes also from library sources), getting interviewees into the studios and writing a script or 'treatment' for the Presenter. The range of tasks undertaken by Researchers at this level is virtually limitless, from finding participants for a quiz show to tracking down an obscure picture or piece of film of a long-forgotten event that is suddenly topical again. Moving beyond the very general duties of this kind, Researchers tend to specialise. In the bigger companies the goal of many is to work on a prestigious network current affairs programme. Here the preparation time is generally measured in weeks or days rather than hours, and much of the work is best described as investigative journalism. Researchers work in teams with the Producer and Programme Director, often travelling extensively with a production unit and sometimes exposed to serious personal risk.

Outside the broad field of current affairs are the more specialised Researcher roles, most of which call for a high level of specialist knowledge and skills. These include research for programmes in such areas as natural history, science, anthropology, music and light entertainment. Drama research, although an identifiable job in television, does not employ significant numbers of people. Much of the research needed for a drama production is done by the Writer, the Designer, and the Make-up and Wardrobe specialists. A significant proportion of Researchers are employed on Children's and Educational programmes.

The majority of Researchers are graduates, although few companies recruit by direct graduate entry. It is normally necessary to have had some post-graduation experience in a media-related area such as newspapers, radio or television. As a body, Researchers tend to be forceful, extrovert, creative and intensely competitive. They may eventually broaden their skills into Producing and Directing and perhaps into Presenting or Journalism.

It is normal practice in the industry for Researchers to be engaged, on a 'run of series' contract. There is significant movement of Researchers between companies, particularly with the true specialists who can work only for a company that is making programmes in their subject area.

Typical Recruitment Profile

Trainee Programme Researcher (General)

	Essential	Desirable
Education and Training	Broad general education, usually to degree standard	Good class of degree. A degree in the appropriate subject is highly desirable for specialised researcher posts.
Experience		Media-related, in newspapers, radio or TV. Knowledge of reference sources. A background in journalism is highly desirable for posts in current affairs, and essential in some companies.
Interests	Broad, embracing the arts, sciences, current affairs, television	

	Essential	*Desirable*
Personal Qualities	Articulate, inquisitive, resourceful, creative, resilient, extrovert and competitive. Able to relate easily to all types of people	

RUNNER

From time to time there may be opportunities for entry to the industry as a Runner. A Runner is the most junior person on the production team and may be asked to assist with a variety of tasks. These may include collecting tapes, looking after artists, helping with administration, etc. It is a useful way to begin to learn about the business and those who are resourceful and inquisitive can gain a great deal from the job. Runners are employed on a short-term basis with no guarantee of renewal of contract. Not all companies employ Runners and vacancies are more likely to occur when a major production is underway.

Enthusiasm, a willingness to help and to learn are the main requirements for the job, together with a proven interest in television production.

SALES AND MARKETING

The Sales Department is a vital part of every ITV programme company. Nearly all of a company's income is derived from the sale of advertising time, and if the Sales Department fails to sell that time, there is no money to make programmes and pay salaries.

Although television is a very effective medium for advertising, the task of the sales staff is not simply to wait for the bookings to come in. They are competing not only with the press and radio, etc. for advertisers, but also with the other ITV companies and increasingly with cable and satellite television stations. Staff must therefore have a very positive approach towards existing television advertisers and towards getting new business.

The ITV companies have sales offices in London. Addresses can be obtained from the company's main site (see 'How to Apply for Jobs in ITV').

Since advertisers wish to reach particular members of the population, perhaps in certain parts of the country, all advertising time is sold on a regional basis by the local ITV station. The exception is Sunrise which, being a national station, has a national sales operation.

Some companies have group sales forces, for example airtime on Anglia, Border and Central is sold by TSMS; at Grampian and HTV by TVMM; and at LWT and TVS (until late 1992) by Laser Sales.

As soon as the ITV network produces its schedule of programmes for the next quarter of the year, the Sales Department can begin to sell the advertising spots or 'airtime'. There are considerable differences between the various sales jobs in the different companies, however, the following general descriptions should be a useful guide.

Sales Co-ordinator

In some companies, these tasks are carried out by Sales Negotiators, Sales Assistants or Sales Executives, but for the sake of simplicity we will refer to Sales Co-ordinators.

The aim of the Sales Co-ordinators is to obtain maximum revenue through the sale of airtime and to ensure that every commercial break is filled with advertisements. They receive bookings over the telephone from advertising agencies or direct from clients, and refer to the computer to see what airtime is available for sale.

In addition, they must take positive action themselves to fill empty spaces, and use their knowledge of airtime availability and advertising campaigns to decide who to contact in the hope of persuading them to buy.

They will discuss overall campaign details and requirements. An agency might, for example, handle a client that sells holidays and wishes to mount a campaign on television from Christmas to March. The Sales Co-ordinator must be aware of any such campaign and be informed as to the size of budget to be spent and the type of person at whom the advertisement is aimed (perhaps in this case women in the middle-income bracket). They will then be able to suggest the best programmes or commercial breaks in which to place the advertisement across the campaign period, subject to availability. The Sales Co-ordinator will book the airtime on the computer and, as time goes on, handle any booking changes that may be required.

Sales Co-ordinators are office-based for most of the time and constantly use a telephone and a computer screen. They must be highly articulate, outgoing and pleasantly persuasive with a good telephone manner. Numeracy is also a vital attribute since it is often necessary to calculate the different rates for advertisements quickly and accurately. A knowledge of ITV programmes, audience research data and current affairs is also needed.

A smart appearance is important as, from time to time, they will meet clients and representatives from agencies. Sales Co-ordinators generally work in teams and will be responsible for a particular group of clients and/or agencies.

Most trainees are appointed in this area, particularly if they have no previous television advertising sales experience. Selling airtime is an ever changing and complex business, as well as being highly competitive. Each company therefore operates its own training scheme, the length of which may vary.

Marketing Executive (or Senior Sales Executive, or Sales Executive)

These staff are responsible for attracting new business to the company and for providing support for existing clients and agencies. They spend less time on the telephone and much more time visiting customers. Their task is to promote the concept of television as an advertising medium and in particular to promote their own company. They may give audio-visual presentations which provide statistics for potential customers to show why they should buy airtime, as well as giving details of the cost of a campaign. They may also discuss how a campaign might be organised. Marketing Executives may have to travel extensively around the United Kingdom, giving promotional talks and generally looking for new business.

The personal qualities that make a good Marketing Executive are similar to those of a good Co-ordinator.

Marketing Executives usually have supervisory responsibility for Sales Co-ordinators.

Market Research Executive (or Sales Researcher)

Market Research is an essential support function for the Sales Department and Programme Makers. The job of the Market Researcher is to collect and interpret market research and media research data for a wide variety of projects.

The Sales Executive may, for example, wish to know how effective television advertising has been in selling breakfast cereals in a certain part of the country so that a new client can be persuaded to mount a campaign. The Market Researcher extracts the data, interprets it and if required prepares it for presentation to the agency and/or client. This could entail the commissioning of original market research which is placed with external research agencies, or the use of the wide variety of syndicated continuous research to compile the necessary report/presentation.

Programme Producers may, for example, want to know what type of people watched their programmes and whether a second series should be commissioned. The Market Researcher may be required to devise questionnaires and brief external Market Research agencies to discover the potential of programmes in question.

Good Market Researchers must be highly numerate in order to interpret data, and sometimes to develop computer models. They may well have to spend long periods with a VDU. The ability to relate easily to staff in other departments and understand their requirements is essential. In some companies, Market Researchers may also be called upon to make formal presentations of their findings to customers, and/or other departments, so all should be able to write clear, concise reports.

Trainees may be appointed as Research Assistants, helping the Market Research Executives in all aspects of their work. Work placements as part of a degree course may also be possible.

Traffic (Make Up Clerk)

One of the chief functions of the Traffic Department is to monitor the 'make up' of the commercial break in the few days before transmission. As the transmission time draws near, traffic staff handle the administration of any last minute bookings.

At this stage it is important to check that the strict rules laid down on advertising by the ITC are being met, although of course staff must always be on the look-out for problems. An actor who is appearing in a programme, for example, must not appear in an advertisement being shown during that programme, and certain advertisements must not be shown within a given time of a children's programme. A good knowledge of ITV programmes is therefore essential. Equally important is a keen interest in current affairs, for example, if there has been an air crash, certain airline advertisements might be in bad taste and the traffic staff would be instructed to ensure that they were withdrawn.

In some companies Traffic staff may also arrange for the collection and delivery of advertisements. They may carry out other duties such as updating the computer on changes to television programmes and entering other data relevant to the sales staff.

Traffic staff spend a great deal of time on the telephone and they must be prepared to work with VDUs. They must be thorough and conscientious in checking the commercial breaks before transmission.

Trainees are generally recruited into Sales Co-ordination, Research or Traffic. In some cases, however, applicants with good A levels, or a degree or equivalent, may be recruited into higher grades (e.g. Trainee Marketing Executive). Some experience of brand selling or in an advertising agency can be useful.

Opportunities exist for promotion through the various grades, or staff may move, say, from Traffic to Sales Co-ordination.

Television Commercials

The ITV companies are responsible only for the transmission of commercials, not for making them. Advertising agencies are responsible for the creative aspects of advertising campaigns, and further details can be found in a useful publication *Getting into Advertising*, which is available from:

The Advertising Association,
Abford House,
15 Wilton Road,
LONDON SW1V 1NJ
Tel: 071 828 2771

Typical Recruitment Profile

Trainee Sales Staff

	Essential	Desirable
Physical	Clean and smart appearance. Acceptable to all types of people. Good clear telephone voice	
Education and Training	Two or more GCE A levels. Subjects not important, but marketing, business studies computer studies, maths, statistics or economics are appropriate	A degree. The subject is not important, but the same subjects are appropriate as for A levels.
Experience		Telephone sales, brand selling or working with an advertising agency.
Interests	A broad range of interests including current affairs and social activities. A knowledge of television programmes	
Personal Qualities	Outgoing and friendly, articulate, numerate. Able to relate to all types of people	Leadership.

SCRIPT EDITOR

There are relatively few people employed as Script Editors in the television industry, and yet the job which they do is both essential and rewarding.

They are nearly all employed in the drama department, working directly for the Producer of a particular programme. Their role is to encourage Writers to develop and express their ideas to the best of their abilities, while ensuring that the Producer's programme needs are met. Experienced Script Editors are usually responsible for commissioning Writers, either alone or with the Producer. Many of these Writers will have a well-established reputation, but Script Editors are always on the look-out for fresh talent and new ideas. Their search will often taken them to fringe theatres, film shows, and to libraries and festivals.

The kind of writer that the Script Editor will look for to write a script for a single play will be very different from the kind of writer needed for a serial. In the former, a number of writers are needed with a mixture of individual ideas perhaps linked by a common theme. They will each contribute a play which will form part of a series. In the latter case, the serial will be originated by one writer, but others will be needed to carry on in the same style over the months and years to follow.

Once the Writer has been commissioned, the Script Editor may be concerned with almost anything to do with the script. There is of course a great deal of administration and correspondence to be done in order to ensure that the script is ready on time, but other duties will depend largely on the way in which the Producer prefers to work.

Some Script Editors carry out research, for example, into historical facts, but this is uncommon in ITV. Some will prepare the 'storyline', liaising with the Producer. This is a rough outline of the story which the Writer then brings alive. Others may carry out 'rewrites' of certain parts of the script if this work is unavoidable, and cannot be done for some reason by the Writer.

Script Editors who are working on serials need an excellent memory. It is their responsibility to advise the Writers on individual characters, their relationships, and who has done what in previous episodes. There would be a considerable outcry from the viewing public if an actor was asked to do something which was out of character, or if an incident was repeated. The Script Editor is therefore responsible for guiding the Writers, moving the story along and for keeping the script within transmission time and budget.

The job requires a very high degree of diplomacy. Everyone can be sensitive to criticism of their work, and Writers are no exception. The Script Editor needs to exercise considerable tact and discretion (as well as forcefulness!) when advising a Writer how to tighten a script, or advising that a particular scene or incident will not work dramatically or visually.

The role is that of a mentor, and the task is to produce a script that has the highest possible dramatic quality. The skill is to be constructive rather than destructive and to encourage rather than stifle creativity.

It is impossible to describe a typical career path into this job since Script Editors come from a variety of sources. A good academic background can help to develop the strong critical faculties that are needed, and a degree in drama, English or a subject related to communications is therefore an advantage.

Experience as a Script Reader for a fringe theatre is also a useful way of developing a sense of judgement and confidence. Script Readers are general paid minimally, but are employed by most theatres to read and prepare reports on the many unsolicited scripts they receive from aspiring Writers. This is a useful way of learning to discriminate between work which is promising and work which is merely run-of-the-mill, and developing the confidence to ensure that you are not going to reject a budding Shakespeare. Script reading for a film or television company is also useful experience, as is a background in journalism. It is unlikely that anyone without a deep interest in drama of all kinds and in communication would be attracted to this kind of work.

Other essential qualities are self-motivation, patience, a willingness to work hard and variable hours, an unquenchable interest in how Writers write, and the ability to work well under sustained pressure.

No recruitment profile is given for this job.

SECRETARY AND CLERK

There is a very wide range of secretarial and clerical posts in the ITV companies and it is impossible to describe here all the openings that may be available. Secretaries and Clerks are employed in almost every department and provide an essential support service in production areas, newsrooms, technical areas, sales, Personnel, Accounts, etc.

Clerks

Junior Clerks are employed in jobs such as handling post, duplicating and printing. More senior Clerks may be employed in posts which carry a fair degree of responsibility such as the booking of BT lines for sending programmes from one station to another, or monitoring the booking of advertisements into commercial breaks. The range of jobs is endless. For those with an aptitude for figures, there are openings in Wages and Accounts departments, and for those who enjoy working with people, there may be openings in Personnel or Production areas.

Some companies ask for a minimum of 5 GCSEs (grades A to C) from applicants for clerical posts and although others do not make this stipulation, it is important to remember that competition for vacancies is tough and qualifications are an advantage. An ability to type and a good telephone manner are also useful in some jobs.

All of the ITV companies look for applicants with good basic common sense, initiative, the ability to work as a member of a team, an interest in the work, and a conscientious attitude. Manual dexterity is very useful as many jobs involve the operation of a computer keyboard.

Junior Secretaries

Applicants for junior secretarial posts should have an accurate typing speed of about 50 words per minute, preferably with an appropriate professional secretarial qualification such as RSA. Previous secretarial experience is not essential, but can be useful. Tasks include filing, dealing with telephone calls, maintaining catalogues, word processing, shorthand or speed writing, audio typing on occasions, and general office duties. Junior Secretaries may work alone, or in a group with other Secretaries and Clerks depending on the nature of the department.

GCSE (grades A to C) or equivalent qualifications are an advantage, and some companies ask for a minimum of five passes. The personal qualities which have been mentioned under the heading of clerical posts are equally important for applicants for all secretarial jobs, both junior and senior.

▓▓ *Secretarial*

Secretaries may work for one person, or for several. They may work alone or in groups. Applicants for more senior positions should be able to organise themselves and the office, use their initiative, and work under considerable pressure from time to time. They should also be able to relate easily to other people, both on the telephone and face to face.

Good educational qualifications are essential and most companies prefer applicants to have 5 GCSEs (grades A to C), or equivalent, preferably including English language. Applicants with GCE A levels, and a degree or business studies qualifications are also welcome, particularly for more senior positions.

Previous secretarial experience is useful for all jobs, and essential for many. Applicants should have an accurate typing speed of 50 words per minute and ideally a shorthand speed of at least 90 words a minute. Experience in the use of word processors and computers is an advantage.

Nearly all vacancies for Trainee Production Assistants are filled by Secretaries from within the companies. In addition, there are some Secretaries who work very closely with the production team. An example is the Producer's Secretary, Production Secretary or Programme Secretary (not employed by every company) who carries out many of the typing functions of the Production Assistant. Programme Secretaries have to become proficient in the transcribing of cassettes containing the sound from filming, so that the film and dialogue can be edited down together. Audio typing is therefore necessary.

Like most staff, Secretaries and Clerks are generally employed on a renewable contract.

No recruitment profile is given for these posts as jobs vary so greatly. In the main, the requirements are no different from those for similar jobs in any industry.

SET DESIGNER

The job of the Designer is one of the most creative in television, and yet it is one which the viewer largely takes for granted. Almost every programme from the studio interview to the prestige drama has a designer whose job is to create the right sense of mood, style, period and place for the programme. The Designer creates the setting within which the action takes place.

Television is a creator of illusions, and so the work of the Designer is not made to last. A solid-looking interior of a house will be made from thin wood, and a dense jungle will be created with a few potted plants. As soon as the recording is finished, the set is dismantled and usually destroyed.

The work of the Television Designer is more complex than that of the Theatre Set Designer. A theatre audience views the set from one angle and from a distance, and sees the set as a whole. A television audience sees the set in close up, in small sections and from many angles, each of which must look equally realistic and cohesive. The job therefore requires meticulous planning, particularly for dramas and light entertainment programmes where the cameras may be required to move around a great deal. Changes in technology are leading to even greater clarity in the picture on the domestic receiver, and this demands a sharpening of all the traditional skills such as attention to finishes, accuracy of detailing and set dressing.

Designers develop their own way of working. Once they have been allocated to a particular programme, for example a drama, they will usually begin by reading the script and translating it into visual terms by drawing sketches. This demands creative interpretation of the Writer's intentions.

The Designer works closely with the Programme Director. Both will have their own ideas on what should be done, but Designers are usually allowed a considerable amount of freedom. They must of course work within a strict budget which is allocated to the programme. They will often draw a 'storyboard' which is rather like a strip

A Set Designer creating a scale model. (*Central TV*)

cartoon, to show the progression of the action and help in the creation of sets. The next step is usually the production of simplified architectual drawings of the sets from which costing estimates can be made by another department. This may be done manually but computer aided design (CAD) systems enable the Designer to plan accurate perspectives of shots that will be available to the Director on the recording day. Ground plans of the studio are also made to ensure that the sets will allow room for cameras and microphone booms to be positioned and moved, for the lighting to be correctly positioned, and for actors and actresses to move around.

There is obviously a great deal of liaison with people in other departments such as the Programme Director, Chief Costume Designer, Lighting Director, Sound Supervisor, etc., and several meetings are held to make sure that all their interests are met. The Designer may produce scale models of the proposed sets for these meetings, and these are of considerable help in ensuring, for example, that a camera can be moved from one position to another without its cables getting in the way.

Once the design of the set has finally been agreed, the construction workshop starts to assemble the scenery, or the basic parts of the set are hired from a specialist firm. Other items are made, hired or bought. Some parts of the set may be 'topped up' or other parts such as ceilings may be added electroncially to the picture after the programme has been recorded. The Designer achieves this by using complex computer graphics equipment.

Designers are responsible not only for the scenery, but for everything else that is on the set such as curtains, furniture, books, carpets, etc. Considerable research is often needed to make sure that the whole effect is authentic, and Designers may spend many hours researching in libraries, museums, etc., before preparing a 'prop list' of required items which they will then obtain from a wide range of sources.

If part of the programme is to be shot away from the studio, the Designer will usually help to find suitable locations, and will take steps to hide any unwanted views. An authentic period cottage, for example, may have a bus-stop outside it which does not fit into the intended period of the programme, and will have to be disguised, or even temporarily removed.

During studio rehearsals, the Designer will supervise the erection of the sets and the 'dressing' of the sets (adding all the extra details). Minor adjustments may also have to be made. When the recording takes place the greater part of the Designer's work is already done and they will probably already have started work on other programmes.

Recruitment is usually as an Assistant Designer. Assistants normally help in the preparation of drawings, models, etc., and in any research that has to be done. They gradually take on more responsibility as experience is gained.

Typical Recruitment Profile

Trainee Assistant Set Designer

	Essential	Desirable
Physical	Good colour vision	
Education and Training	BA in Interior Design or BA in Art and Design or architecture degree or BA Stage Design	
Experience	Draughting	Commercial art studio, interior design, theatre design, architecture.
Interests	Three dimensional design architectural styles, contemporary design, period furniture, fashion trends	Theatre, television, films.
Personal Qualities	Ability to communicate ideas. Highly creative	

SOUND TECHNICIAN

In a medium which is dominated by the picture, the contribution of sound is often underestimated by the viewer and yet programmes without theme music, background music and sound effects, let alone dialogue, would be unthinkable.

The great majority of programmes are made on tape, and the emphasis here is on taped productions. The operational and artistic skills which are required by the sound specialist are very similar regardless of whether tape or film is used.

Studio Sound

The early years of a Sound Technician's career are normally spent in the studio gaining a thorough grounding in studio sound operations on the studio floor. A period of familiarisation may also be spent in the sound control room.

One of the first skills to be grasped is that of operating the boom. The boom microphone is mounted on the end of a telescopic arm which in turn is mounted on a dolly. This is moved around the studio to follow the action. Good hand-eye co-ordination is necessary, together with an understanding of camera angles and studio lighting. Incorrect positioning of the boom will not only produce poor perspective sound, but may cast unwanted shadows from the lights across the picture. This can result in a costly retake of a scene.

Sound Technicians will learn the characteristics and uses of the various other types of microphone in the studio, and how to place them correctly. They will also be responsible for ensuring that the communication systems such as 'talkback' between the studio and control room, as well as loud-speakers, etc., are working.

Sound Mixer

A variety of duties are carried out in the Sound Control Room including the monitoring and adjusting of sound levels during recording. The staff who work here are generally more experienced, and include the Sound Mixer, who is normally a Supervisor. Sound Mixers are responsible for the crew working for them and for the operation of the audio mixer console or 'sound desk'. This consists of a vast array of buttons and switches, each of which is concerned with an incoming sound source. There may be typically 24 separate sound sources or as many as 56 which the Sound Mixer can fade up or down, and mix and balance to produce the desired output for the programme. The Sound Mixer will also correct deficiencies in the original sound as far as possible.

Grams Operator

One of the sources feeding into the sound desk will be from the Grams Operator, who has a library of sound effects and music. These are held either on tape or on compact disc. On cue from the Director, the Grams Operator will play the appropriate material into the programme, and the Sound Mixer will make any necessary adjustments.

During live transmissions such as News and Current Affairs, Grams Operators may be required to work on their own initiative selecting appropriate music and effects for the programme. Creativity and good aural perception are essential for this. The Grams Operator must also be able to edit tape under the kind of pressure caused by tight deadlines.

Post-Production Sound

Once the programme has been recorded, the finishing touches are put to the sound in 'post-production'. The picture will have been edited, and re-assembled into its final form and, if left untouched, there would probably be jumps and discrepancies in the accompanying sound tracks. The technicians in post-production sound or dubbing re-assemble and even re-record the sound track to fit the picture. They may also add special sound effects which were not included during recording, as well as the opening and closing theme tunes for the programme. Occasionally there may be an unwanted sound such as aircraft on the original sound track. This must be removed or disguised so that the viewer is unaware of what has happened.

Attention to fine detail is essential. It may be necessary to match the voice recordings of one artist made in say 23 different locations, each of which has different acoustics.

Experienced Sound Technicians with proven artistic and creative abilities are normally selected for these positions.

Outside Broadcasts and Location Shoots

All of the duties which have been described so far are equally important on location although the equipment used may be slightly different, and there are some different challenges to be faced. Whereas in the studio much of the equipment is fixed, every facility to be found on an OB or location has to be set up and made to work by the crew on the day and then stripped out after the event. This may have to be done in darkness or rain.

Sound Technicians tend to have a variety of responsibilities for sound on location and specialist knowledge is needed, for example, to

A Sound Technician on location for Granada Television. (*Granada TV*)

cope with the wind blowing against microphones or gathering sound effects over wide areas and long distances. The Sound crew is also responsible for communications back to the studio, which are often extremely complicated.

Maintenance

The responsibility for the maintenance and technical alignment of the sound equipment varies from company to company. In some cases, these tasks are carried out by engineers in a separate maintenance section, whilst in others it is the responsibility of the Sound Technician to carry out at least basic maintenance. Equipment on location often has to be fixed on the spot and in a hurry because the crew is many miles from base and replacements cannot be obtained quickly.

Current Developments

Each of the tasks mentioned above has tended in the past to be a separate function and the Sound Technician progressed through most, if not all, over a period of years. Changes in technology and operational practice mean, however, that many of the functions are combining. In many companies there is a change in emphasis away from technical expertise towards greater creativity and artistic appreciation in sound. Sound may also be combined with other functions such as Cameras and Editing, particularly on location.

There are exciting times ahead in television. Stereo television is being introduced and many companies are looking seriously at digital audio throughout the broadcast chain.

Typical Recruitment Profile

Trainee Sound Technician

	Essential	Desirable
Physical	Normal colour vision. Acute aural perception. Quick, calm, ear-hand reactions	
Education and Training	Broad general education to at least GCSE (grades A to C) standard including maths and prefereably physics	(1) BTEC/City & Guilds/HND/ Degree in electronics, computer science or communications or (2) BA Tonmeister or (3) Film and TV course at College of FE.
Interests	Flair for some aspect of audio work, e.g., musical performance or	Wide interest in film and television. Electronics as a hobby.

Essential	*Desirable*
recording, or public address work. The modern music scene. A knowledge of musical notation is essential for operational aspects of sound	

SPECIAL EFFECTS

The term 'special effects' covers an enormous range of techniques carried out by many different people using anything from a piece of string to a computer. It can perhaps be described as 'distortion of reality'.

Very few people indeed are employed full-time on special effects in ITV and they are only found in some of the largest companies. For many staff in TV, the creation of effects is a part of their job, but many effects are commissioned from outside companies which specialise in this field.

To most people, the term special effects brings to mind spectacular sequences in a Steven Spielberg film or a television advertisement but this is only a very small part of the story. Effects fall roughly into two categories – those that are physically built or made, and those that are generated electronically on a computer. The latter are used increasingly in television, but the decision on which method to use will depend upon the degree of reality that can be achieved, on the cost and to a degree, on fashion. A company specialising in computer-generated effects, for example, turned down a request to create a sequence in which a pterodactyl was to fly around the Royal Albert Hall. This could be achieved electronically, but it would not look as realistic as it would if a model pterodactyl was built. There are fashions for electronic effects, and indeed for reality. A television commercial which showed a car being driven through a field of burning crops, was film in reality without any special effects. Physical effects such as models, puppets, and explosions, and 'optical' effects such as back projection and split mirrors are normally created by specialist companies working primarily for the film industry. There are probably no more than two or three people working full-time in this area in ITV. The work is enormously varied and is limited only by the imagination. The Programme Director and the Set Designer will describe what they want to achieve, and it is the task of the specialist to create that effect in the way that looks most realistic and unstaged within the budget allowed for the task. This calls for a great deal of ingenuity and persistence, trying things out again and again using different techniques and materials until it works. There are few rules to follow. Many techniques are passed on by work of mouth or by inquisitively working out how someone else has achieved an effect. You need to be pushy, cheeky, single-minded, and a determined perfectionist. Some things may be learned the hard way, such as how to create a house fire without burning down the building! The use of fire and explosives (pyrotechnics) can be dangerous and there are certain rules on safety which must be followed. It is important to remember that in the area of 'physical' special effects, you may have responsibility for people's lives.

There is no clearly defined career path to follow. Some specialists have begun their careers as Electricians, or in the Props Department, both of which can provide relevant skills. A background in subjects as diverse as engineering and/or sculpture is useful for example in model making and in puppet making. A knowledge of mechanics is useful if you are to 'rig up' a special effect such as a tyre bursting on a car. Practical skills are clearly important, but they will be of little value unless combined with creativity, artistic ability and the skill of thinking laterally as well as logically. Many people tend to specialise in the use of a certain medium according to their particular skills and interests.

There is no set pattern of promotion in this field. You do the job because you love it, and are happy to spend your nights lying awake trying to work out how to overcome a problem.

Video effects, i.e. those which are created electronically by computer, are also made predominantly by specialist companies working outside the ITV network. They provide a service to the broadcast companies but also to the makers of television commercials, promotional videos and many others. The service they offer is primarily at the 'post-production' stage. Once the programme has been recorded by an ITV company, for example, it is sent to the specialist organisation or 'facility house' to have the video effects added.

Once again, it is difficult to describe adequately the kind of effects that can be produced since they are limited only by imagination and the capability of the computer. The Channel 4 logo and the introductory sequence to ITN's News at Ten are examples of video effects. Such effects are created on a variety of computer graphics equipment most of which have slightly different capabilities. Some are capable of producing a three-dimensional effect, giving the impression of light, waves, ripples, etc. Many advertisements use video effects. Some incorporate video effects, physical effects and reality superimposed on each other, and involve co-operation between several different companies.

Some video effects are added 'live' to television programmes, for example, the live pictures from a light entertainment show can be fed instantly down a communications line to a video effects company. The company offers appropriate effects to the Programme Director back in the control room. The effects appear on a screen in front of the Director and are added to the live programme as appropriate.

There is no set career path into video effects. Some would argue that a background in electronics engineering is useful in order to understand how the computer graphics equipment operates. Other employers look for computing specialists and will only accept people who can programme the computer using the appropriate language. In some cases the video effects specialist is required to programme the computer and in some cases not. Some have a background in the sciences, for example a degree in physics, while others have a background in the arts. It is not necessary to have a degree in any of the subjects mentioned, however many people do, and the competition for jobs often means that a degree is an advantage.

A logical mind is, however, vital and must be combined with a high level of creativity and artistic flair.

Jobs are rarely advertised. Those within the ITV companies are normally filled internally, while those in specialist facility companies are often filled by people who have started at the bottom as runners, or who have turned up on the doorstep at the right time.

We have looked so far at people who are employed full-time on special effects, but for many different staff in ITV, special effects form a part of their job. The Make-up Artist for example may be called upon to produce special effects such as ageing a character, or turning a man into a werewolf. The Vision Mixer will create video effects such as splitting the screen or spinning the picture, and the work of the Graphic Designer will incorporate many video effects using the same computer graphics equipment mentioned above. The Props department may from time to time be called upon to build, for example, a magic castle for a children's programme. Video Editors, Lighting Directors, Costume Designers, and almost everyone involved in the creative aspects of programme making will be concerned with special effects from time to time.

A career in special effects is exciting, challenging and possibly one of the most creative there is. As one specialist put it, it is 'living out everyone else's fantasies'.

No recruitment profile is given for this job.

STAGEHAND AND PROPS

Another very interesting area of work in television is handling scenery and properties. Stagehands, Scenehands or Setting Assistants are the people who erect the scenery in the studio or on location after it has been made by the craftsmen. Their job is very similar to that of stagehands in the theatre. Scenery for the most part consists of large 'flats' made of plywood mounted on wooden battens. It has to be assembled piece by piece and is fastened together and supported by all manner of clips, ties, braces and struts. Stagehands are skilled at interpreting the Designer's floor plan and drawings in order to erect the sets in exactly the right part of the studio or location. They work in small teams putting up the set, working some special effects, captions and any scenery changes during the show, then dismantling and removing the scenery to store after the recording or transmission is over.

The Property staff, known as 'Props' do a similar job to the Stagehands except that they are concerned with all the 'action props' used by the artistes, e.g., cutlery, crockery, food, drinks, cigarettes, telephones, pianos – the list is endless. They may also do some driving, for example when cars are used as props they may move them to and from the location. Some may also drive other vehicles associated with the production (but not during the shoot). In most companies the jobs of Stagehand and Props are combined.

Within the Properties Department, Propmakers are sometimes employed. These are the people who manufacture the models or fake structures needed for special visual effects. They work in a variety of material such as papier mâché and fibreglass to create realistic scale models of buildings, ships, machinery, in fact anything that the Writer's and Designer's imaginations may dream up. It should be noted though, that the really spectacular special effects associated with science fiction thrillers are normally the work of highly skilled specialists hired in for the production. Many of the more routine props are hired from outside contractors.

Both Stagehands' and Props' work is for much of the time very strenuous requiring both physical strength and stamina. Long and irregular hours are worked and in most companies location work is a regular duty. The skills of a Stagehand can be acquired by any reasonably fit and intelligent person with the ability to learn to read drawings and tie fancy knots. Propmakers' vacancies are usually filled from the experienced Prophand/Stagehands' ranks, when an artistic eye and/or craft skills may be sought. Some Stage and Props Hands go on to become Property Buyers which is a very specialised job.

Unless genuine opportunities for advancement exist, a creatively ambitious person would be well advised to avoid seeking a Stagehand's job as a means of entering the Industry. But for anyone who likes to be physically active and has a taste for, and preferably some experience of, behind-the-scenes stage work the life of a Stage or Prophand can be very satisfying.

Typical Recruitment Profile

Trainee Stage/Prophand

	Essential	Desirable
Physical	Strong, fit, with good stamina	
Education and Training		Clean driving licence. HGV licence.
Interests	Stagework, music, any crafts	

TECHNICAL OPERATOR

One of the best ways of starting a career in ITV for those with both a technical and an artistic flair, is as a Trainee Technical Operator. Technical Operators are employed in the operation of a wide range of sound and vision equipment in production and post-production.

Many companies recruit Trainee Technical Operators from time to time although the precise nature of the training will differ according to the areas to be covered. The length of the traineeship varies from about six months to two years depending on the number of departments in which training is given, and the level of skill expected. During the first few months, trainees will be attached to a variety of departments for perhaps four to six weeks at a time. This gives them a broad understanding of the operation of a television station. Later, they will specialise in one area where they have demonstrated particular aptitude, and where vacancies for Technical Operators are likely to exist.

Most of the training is very practical with structured experience under supervision. From time to time trainees may attend relevant short courses to strengthen their understanding.

The areas in which Technical Operators are most commonly employed are as follows:

Vision Control

In the suite of control rooms associated with each studio is an operational desk controlling the colour balance and exposure of each of the studio cameras. The technician allocated to this duty ensures that each 'shot' is correctly adjusted, and liaises closely with the Lighting Director (usually in the same control room) to ensure that the video output from the studio is both technically and artistically satisfactory. In some studio centres, video tape recorders are also controlled from this operational position.

The vision control staff may carry out maintenance on cameras, while in other companies this responsibility is delegated to separate central apparatus room staff or a maintenance department.

Vision control room at Central Television. (*Central TV*)

Video Tape Recording (VTR or VT)

The VTR section is a prime component of any television centre and carries a high operational workload. The section has two main functions.

The first of these is to edit programmes which have been recorded on video tape. A separate section of the book describes the role of the Editor in detail.

The second is to record programmes as they are made in the studio, relay recorded inserts into live programmes, replay programmes for transmission, and to 'time shift' programmes which may be required to be transmitted at different times throughout the United Kingdom.

VTR transmissions at Central Television. (*Central TV*)

Staff who join the VT department are normally concerned with recording and replaying programmes. Those with creative ability may progress into editing as opportunities arise.

In some companies, VT staff are also responsible for the maintenance of their equipment.

▓ *Telecine*

Although most television programmes are made and transmitted on video tape, a sizeable minority are made on film and then transferred to tape. In addition, many cinema movies are of course shown on television. The telecine machine is designed to convert film into a television signal for transmission which it does by 'scanning' each shot. The task of the operational engineer or technician in the telecine department is to obtain the most satisfactory audio and video output from the equipment.

Colour grading telecine film at Granada Television. (*Granada TV*)

Cine film is a medium far from ideally suited to reproduction on television due to its wide contrast range and varying colour rendition. Telecine staff can correct these aberrations with sophisticated electronic processors. The need to cope with a variety of film gauges, cinemascope, widescreen and stereo sound tracks adds complexity and interest to this operation.

As in VTR, the responsibility for the maintenance and technical alignment of the equipment may lie within the department, or with a separate maintenance section.

Central Apparatus Room (CAR)

The Central Apparatus Room is the nerve centre of the studio complex. In it is housed a large proportion of the electronics providing routing of video and audio signals throughout the station. Much of the video mixing, processing and digital effects equipment is also housed here, as is the equipment providing central timing and test signals.

This area is the communications hub between areas within the studio complex, to other ITV companies, to the transmitters and to BT who provide communication lines.

Technicians working in this area are responsible for the monitoring and, where necessary, the correction of the technical parameters of all audio and video sources within the complex. In particular, they are responsible for incoming signals from other centres and the routing of those signals to the transmitter.

Outside Broadcasts

Many television programmes are transmitted from, or recorded at, locations away from the studio centres. The control rooms and electronic equipment used in these circumstances are fitted within 'outside broadcast vehicles' sometimes known as 'scanners'.

The Technicians employed with these scanners perform similar duties to those already mentioned. However, the absence of base support and the need to work under frequently difficult environmental conditions often place greater emphasis on the individual's initiative and motivation.

Radio Links

When it is necessary to transmit an outside broadcast live from location, circuits for vision, music and communications are required back to the studio centre. Occasionally permanent landlines are available, but in most instances the vision and music circuits are carried by a temporary microwave radio link.

A typical link would consist of a vehicle adjacent to the outside broadcasting location, housing a microwave transmitter and communications equipment. The aerial for this transmitter would be mounted either at the top of the vehicle's mast, on the vehicle roof, or dismounted from the vehicle and rigged on a suitable roof top.

The 'receive' point for the link may be a permanently installed aerial located on a transmitter mast or high building. Alternatively it may be another links vehicle on a remote hilltop which receives and re-transmits (mid-point) the signal to a further receive point, or feeds the signals into the permanent ITV lines network.

A Granada links vehicle on location. (*Granada*)

The microwave frequencies used for these links require structured 'line of sight' transmission paths to ensure that satisfactory circuits are provided for the broadcast. Ideally the route should be carefully surveyed by the Radio Links Engineers in advance, to check for obstructions such as hills or high buildings, or other problems. There are times, particularly in news operations, when links are required at very short notice from locations which have not previously been used or surveyed. On these occasions the engineer must use initiative and experience to establish a usable link.

Technicians working on radio links are required to rig equipment under adverse weather conditions and often at heights. Considerable self-reliance, resourcefulness and determination are called for.

Camera Operations • Sound Operations • Vision Mixing

For details of the tasks involved in the last three of these areas, please refer to the relevant sections of this book.

Technical Operators must feel at ease with the operation of equipment. They should also have sufficient aptitude for engineering to be able to carry out first-line or basic maintenance after training and to understand the principles behind the operations they are carrying out. An artistic flair is equally important since all of the jobs contribute in varying degrees to the look, feel or sound of the final programme.

Technical Operators work alongside Engineers in many areas and for those who have a strong interest and relevant qualifications in engineering there may well be an opportunity to transfer. Others may prefer to develop their career in the more creative areas of production.

Typical Recruitment Profile

Trainee Technical Operator

	Essential	Desirable
Physical	Ear-hand-eye co-ordination. Good colour vision	
Education and Training	Broad general education to at least GSCE standard (grades A to C) including maths and English. Degree or equivalent in engineering or computer science related subject for those wishing to progress to pure engineering posts	A level standard in maths and/or physics. BTEC ONC/ OND/City and Guilds in electronics, computer science or communications.
Interests	Wide range of technical team work and media and arts related interests	

TRANSMISSION CONTROLLER/ PRESENTATION CONTROLLER

The work of a television station falls very broadly into two areas. On the one hand there are the Producers, Directors, Camera Operators, Sound Technicians, Editors, etc., who make programmes which, in the main, are stored away for future use.

On the other hand, there are the staff who are responsible for the station's output of programmes on that particular day. Some staff such as technicians, journalists, etc., are involved in both aspects of the station's work, but a small number of staff are concerned more or less exclusively with the day's schedule of programmes, and it is this aspect of television that we are concerned with here.

The more traditional role of Transmission Controllers is to send the output of programmes in sequence, and on time to the local IBA transmitter. They are the last link between the station and the public and as such have a vital role to play. The station's image with the public depends not only on the quality of the programmes but also on the smooth progression from programme to commercials, to announcements, to news flashes, etc. It is the Transmission Controller's responsibility to ensure that this is done. If a Director makes a mistake while recording a programme, the scene can be re-shot, but if the Transmission Controller makes a mistake the result is there for the viewing public to see.

The working environment of the Transmission Controller can, appear somewhat daunting at first to the outsider. There is a large presentation mixer console covered with buttons, switches and lights, and a bank of television monitors showing such things as the picture going from the station to the transmitter, the picture going from the transmitter to the home, and the start of the next programme in sequence. The room is permanently darkened and the Transmission Controller is unlikely to see daylight for many hours.

One of the most important pieces of equipment in the room is the clock, since the Transmission Controller must press the appropriate switches to bring in the next commercial, programme, or announcement on the second. Split second timing is vital because of the Network system by which ITV operates. Any one of the ITV stations might be the originator of a programme which is sent on cue via a land line or other form of link to the other stations. From there the

Transmission Controller sends it on to the local transmitter. At the same time all commercials originate from the local station, as do local news programmes and announcements. Co-ordination is essential. If the Transmission Controller fails to react quickly the region might miss, for example, the start of News at Ten.

It follows that the job involves a considerable amount of planning and preparation before the start of a shift. The Transmission Controller must, for example, be thoroughly familiar with the planned programme schedule, where programmes will originate, which commercials are to be transmitted and their exact length, which back-up programmes are available in the event of a problem and if any news items are likely to cause a break in the planned schedule. A thorough knowledge of IBA rules on what can and cannot be transmitted is also essential.

The job combines hectic activity and pressure with periods of relative inactivity between commercial breaks, however, concentration is vital at all times in case something goes wrong. If there is a technical failure in the middle of a film, for example, it is the Transmission Controller who must ensure that the public is not left with a blank screen. It is a mixture of teamwork, working alone, and of periods of intense stress and apparent inactivity.

The job requires an intelligent, quick thinking approach combined with a high degree of manual dexterity. In addition, editorial perception and a good visual sense are needed. Many Transmission Controllers have been skilled typists, telegraphists and sound mixers. They are quick to make decisions, have good spatial perception, speed of response – and a liking for the detail of administration.

Many trainee vacancies are filled internally by staff from a variety of departments.

The role of the Transmission Controller is however changing rapidly with the introduction of new technology which enables many of the traditional tasks to be carried out automatically. The job is therefore often combined with others in the technical operations field.

In a few companies the Transmission Controller's role has evolved into that of a 'Presentation Director'. The Presentation Director, in addition to transmission control duties may also be involved in such things as the producing, directing and scheduling of on-screen promotions for forthcoming programmes.

Typical Recruitment Profile

Trainee Assistant Transmission Controller

	Essential	*Desirable*
Physical	Excellent hand-eye co-ordination. Quick reactions. Good, clear speech	
Education	Broad general education to at least GCSE (grades A to C) standard	A levels or degree (any subject).
Interests	Interest in television. Good knowledge of current affairs and well informed on the broad ranges of topics covered by television programmes	
Personal Qualities	High degree of concentration. Ability to work in isolation for long periods. Initiative under pressure. Equable temperament	

VISION MIXER

The Vision Mixer's job is to assemble sequences of visual images from various sources during the making of a television programme. It is a job which combines operating skills with artistic interpretation and is a vital part of the production process.

The pictures which make up a programme come from a variety of sources, for example, from cameras in the studio, pre-recorded video tape, from a 'telecine' machine (which transfers film into a television picture), or from slide photographs. All of these sources are available to the Programme Director who must decide which ones to use and in what order.

If we look at the example of a news programme, the Director may decide to start with a shot of the main Presenter in the studio on camera one, then cut to a shot of the second Presenter on camera two, followed by a video tape illustrating the news, and finally a slide photograph of a person associated with the story. It is the task of the Vision Mixer to make the cuts from one source to the next at the appropriate moment, interpreting the wishes of the Director. The job is in essence 'live' picture editing.

The cuts are made on a complex electronic machine known as the vision mixing console which is located in the studio control room. All the vision sources are fed into the console and as the Vision Mixer operates the controls the end result is recorded onto video tape, or transmitted live according to the programme.

The vision mixing console can also produce special effects to make the transition from one source to another more interesting. It can, for example, fade one picture into the next or 'wipe' from one picture to another. The complexity of consoles varies considerably, but some are capable of digital effects such as spinning the picture around or dividing the screen into a pattern of small pictures. This can produce an attractive result on a light entertainment show, for example.

Vision Mixers also work on outside broadcasts such as church services, sports events, etc. Each outside broadcast vehicle is equipped with a vision mixing console, usually with fairly limited capabilities, however, not all OBs require the services of a Vision Mixer.

A good Vision Mixer will be able to anticipate when the Director will give the cue to make the cut. This is important because the exact moment at which the cut is made can be critical and a slow reaction to a cue can ruin the desired effect. A badly timed cut can spoil the mood of a sequence. Similarly in musical programmes it is important that the cut is made exactly on the right beat. Very quick reactions, artistic judgement, a sense of rhythm and a feel for music are therefore essential.

Although the modern vision mixing console is a very sophisticated piece of equipment it is not necessary to be an electronics expert in order to operate it. It does however employ advanced digital electronic techniques and it can be an advantage to develop a feel for the logic in order to get the maximum performance from the machine.

Vision Mixers spend most of their working day in the control room which is dark. They must be able to concentrate on television monitors for long periods, carry ideas in their heads and follow instructions quickly and accurately. They must also be able to work under considerable physical and mental pressure from time to time. Manual dexterity is important in order to locate and press the correct buttons on the console.

The job may sometimes be combined with Directing, especially on straight-forward programmes.

Trainee Vision Mixers are usually recruited from amongst the existing staff of the television companies. No particular background experience is specified and applicants come from a wide variety of jobs in television including technical, administrative and secretarial. Very occasionally, trainee Vision Mixers may be recruited externally, but this is the exception rather than the rule.

Typical Recruitment Profile

Trainee Vision Mixer

	Essential	*Desirable*
Physical	Good colour vision. Excellent hand-eye and hand-ear co-ordination. Manual dexterity	
Education and Training	Broad, general education to at least GCSE (grades A to C).	Film and/or Television production course. Basic knowledge of geometry is an advantage in operating digital video effects.
Experience		Working with a computer.

	Essential	*Desirable*
		Experience of working in some aspect of television is highly desirable. Able to read musical scores.
Interests		Television, theatre, amateur dramatics, music, visual arts.
Personal Qualities	Quick reactions. Able to follow instructions quickly and accurately. High degree of concentration. Able to keep calm under pressure for long periods. Artistic and musical appreciation	

WRITER

Television Scriptwriters are normally employed on a freelance basis for a particular programme or series. The education, training and experience of Writers is very varied as there is no set career path to follow, and it is therefore only possible to provide very general information here.

A sound educational background, especially in literary subjects such as English and possibly foreign literature is a firm basis from which to begin but no specific qualifications are required. Many universities and colleges of higher education offer courses in creative writing, either as part of a broader full-time course, or as specific short courses. There are also evening classes both in general writing and specifically for radio, film and television. Details of such courses can be obtained from the universities and colleges, local arts associations and education establishments. You may also find details at your local library of writing circles where people who are interested in writing can obtain advice and criticism – essential ingredients in all creative work.

A lucky few may break into television scriptwriting by writing an original piece and sending it unsolicited to television companies. Others may prefer to seek out a reputable literary agent who can find a suitable customer for their work. Agents will of course require fees for their services.

Fresh, new ideas are always very welcome, however, potential Scriptwriters should also bear in mind that in order to earn a living they may have to respond to other people's ideas. They may for example be asked to write a script for a long-running soap opera. This will mean creating new situations for well-established characters in a style which blends in with that of previous writers. Other writers may be employed to adapt well-known books into a format which is suitable for television.

Comedy scriptwriting is a specialised skill, and established comedy writers are commissioned to write scripts for series in much the same way as drama Scriptwriters. It is however possible to begin by submitting single jokes for consideration by specific comedians. It is clearly necessary to tailor the joke to the particular style of the comedian. Some comedy Scriptwriters are lucky enough to begin their careers by having complete programme scripts accepted by a television company, but this is comparatively rare.

Scriptwriting is a very speculative profession and often very insecure. It is subject to current vogues, fashions and topical demands and successful writers will anticipate these rather than merely write what appeals to them. It is also very important to remember that scripts must be suitable for the visual medium. Writers often have to face numerous rejections and strong criticism which can be very discouraging. Perseverance and tenacity are essential charactertistics as well as creativity and writing skills.

There are opportunities for Welsh, Gaelic and other ethnic minority writers to meet the demand for programmes for various cultural groups.

No recruitment profile is given for this job.

OTHER JOBS

There are a number of jobs within television which are highly specialised and which are rarely available as direct entry points to the Industry. It is also very difficult to advise on the kind of background that is needed for these posts. Luck, chance, and being in the right place at the right time are the important ingredients.

▓▓ *Casting*

Not all of the ITV Companies have a Casting Department, but those that do normally employ Casting Directors at a senior level and Booking Assistants at the junior level (although titles may vary).

Prior experience in the acting profession is usually required. Typical previous experience might be employment in a large theatrical agency.

▓▓ *Continuity*

The job of Continuity does not exist as a separate entity in television as it does in the film industry. Responsibility for ensuring that the visual flow from one scene to the next is correct lies with the Production Assistant, but forms only a small part of the job.

▓▓ *Grips*

These are specialists who rig scaffolding and camera rails, special camera cranes and mountings. The job title comes from the Film Industry and where TV productions require them they are generally hired in from specialist companies. Some ITV companies now train their own but they are always recruited internally, normally from Stagehands and Rigger/Drivers. The use of Portable Single Camera (PSC) has led to more location work and so to a few more opportunities for Grips in ITV.

▓▓ *Production Buyers*

Production Buyers or Property Buyers are responsible for purchasing items needed for inclusion in programmes. They work closely with the Set Designers in order to purchase appropriate furniture, food, greenery, books, or anything else that is needed as a prop. They rely heavily on personal contacts, so experience of the Industry is essential. Entry to the job tends to be either from the Props Department, or from theatrical stage management.

Sports Associates

These are usually experienced television Journalists who also have a deep interest in sport and have been lucky enough to be able to combine the two. Very few people are employed in these posts.

Weather Reporter

Many of the Weather Reporters who are responsible for the main weather forecasts are qualified meteorologists who came into contact with television through their work with the Meteorological Office. Some however are individuals with no previous expertise in meteorology who have been identified by the television company as having the right qualities to present the weather forecast. They usually have some experience in the media.

INDEX